Cedar + Salt

Cedar + Salt

Vancouver Island Recipes from Forest, Farm, Field, and Sea

DL ACKEN AND
EMILY LYCOPOLUS

TOUCHWOOD

To James, who, more than
anything or anyone else,
makes this beautiful place
where we live feel like home.

—DANIELLE

To Grandpa Russel,
Grandma Phoebe, and Mom.
You instilled in me a love
for this island that only
continues to grow. Thank you
for calling this place home.

—EMILY

Contents

Introduction

On a hot and dry mid-August day, I stood on the side of a quiet country road, picking and eating blackberries. I'd pick one for me, then one for the bucket. Then I'd pick two for me, and one for the bucket. At the age of five, I thought this approach worked well.

My family often visited my grandparents in Mill Bay, where we would forage for blackberries; it was, in fact, our tradition. The abundance of wild blackberries on Vancouver Island was and continues to be mind-boggling—we would fill buckets until the buckets overflowed, and still we would add even more. We knew the bucket was really full when the berries started settling and the weight of the ones on top crushed the bottom ones into juice.

Back at Grandma's house, the berries from the tops of the buckets would be frozen on cookie sheets, then transferred to freezer bags for a winter indulgence, when I would savour them while dreaming of those hot summer days. The juicy berries at the bottom were transformed into succulent pies, blackberry apple jam, and preserves. The smell from all the baking and processing filled my grandma's kitchen with an intoxicating aroma, and it was there that I fell in love with Vancouver Island.

Ever since then I have felt lucky to have roots in this unique and incredible place. The bounty that Vancouver Island provides is astounding: The cool, wet, misty winters create the perfect environment for kale and Swiss chard to grow year-round; the south-facing slopes of the Cowichan Valley are perfect for growing citrus, olives, and all sorts of exotic foods you'd be surprised to find in Canada; in the sheltered coves, crabs and prawns flourish; in the deep waters and rivers, salmon spawn.

Living off the land and cultivating a holistic, sustainable lifestyle is not only attainable on Vancouver Island, it's a way of life available to all. Why get food from off the Island that has to be delivered to us by boat or plane when the prices found at local farmers markets are often on par with the grocery stores? Purchasing and supporting local producers is simple and rewarding, and grows a bustling local food economy. Here you can stroll through farmers markets in the summer, learn from passionate growers about their multicoloured carrots and purple peppers, and find classified ads that invite people to pick overly abundant apple or fig trees. I want to share this bounty and help you bring it home to your own kitchen. In these pages, I invite you to join me in the adventure of living and eating on this coast. We are incredibly blessed to live here, and my heart's desire is to share with you the meaning of living, cooking, and eating on Canada's Vancouver Island. —EL

When I was a young girl, I thought the Old Island Highway went on forever, a long, seemingly endless, winding road. My family's weekly journey from the Departure Bay ferry terminal to our cottage in Deep Bay regularly included the same, much-anticipated stops: a farm stand in Nanoose, where we'd buy greens and other field veggies; Parksville, for ice cream; Qualicum Village, for cheese and other assorted gourmet goodies and then a seafood lunch at the beach; Bowser for local bacon, eggs, and the ever-important fishing bait. It would take hours to reach our destination, but when we did we were laden with local goods, and our weekend routine could commence.

Dad would always start our Saturdays at the unimaginable hour of 4 AM. With smiles and hot tea, he would shuffle us out to the boat, telling us, "this is when the fish wake up," and I suppose I believed him because we were usually one of the only pleasure crafts in a sea of commercial boats heading out of the harbour to set our lines early and catch our fill before lunchtime. At a young age, I learned the best fishing practices throughout the Broughton Sound: head out at the crack of dawn for coho salmon along the lighthouse shore, then over to Norris Rocks in the lazy noonday sun for ling cod and other assorted rockfish, and then check the traps on the way home for a lucky catch of Dungeness crab. (Continued on page 14)

introduction

introduction

(Continued from page 10) Sometimes Dad would set up the little boat barbecue, and our lunch would come out of the sea and into the pan within three to four minutes of being caught. It was the freshest and most delicious fish you can imagine. Afterward, we'd head in for lazy walks along the shores of Fanny Bay, where Dad would scoop up oysters off the rocks and pop them open to slurp down their creamy flesh and briny liquor, being careful not to crunch into one of the few beautiful pearls he would sometimes hand to me. Then we'd go back to the cabin for leisure time, a stroll down to the marina store, or, in the high summer, endless hours of berry picking and foraging in the small ravine beside the house. If we were lucky, Dad would take us up to Comox for dinner at The Old House where local beef was on the menu.

This was my childhood away from school and the normal comings and goings of life in the city. These trips planted the seeds for a lifetime connection between place and food, which took root and grew deep within my being. Now, when I think about those places on the Island, there is a direct link in my brain between their names and the flavours that come along with them: Parksville and Coombs are dairy-rich and sweet, like ice cream; Qualicum is salty, like its glorious cheese and clams and freshly baked bread; Deep Bay, Fanny Bay, and Union Bay are briny like the oysters and fish they harbour; and the Comox Valley is fertile and hearty, like its grass-fed beef.

Long before the new inland highway began to shuttle goods at lightning speed up and down Vancouver Island, people looked locally for these foods, always readily available around them. Importing from the Mainland can be expensive, thus meats reared at local farms, vegetables swapped for eggs over neighbouring fences, and a bounty of readily available seafood became staples of the daily diet of those who call this Island home. Now, as an adult living and raising my children here, I've come to appreciate how vast these local ingredients are. When you add locally sourced grains, citrus, wines, wild game, and seafood to the list, you'll get an idea of how impressive our food options are on Vancouver Island.

I invite you to join us for a ride as we meander along the Old Island Highway, rest quietly through the storms in Port Renfrew and Tofino, and get lost on the back roads of Sooke, Metchosin, and the Cowichan and Comox Valleys. This Island is vast in flavours, rich in ingredients and culinary innovation—and it's all right here, just waiting for you to enjoy. —DLA

introduction

field

What comes out of a Canadian field? When you give some thought to it, the variety, volume, and complexity of Canada's cultivated crops are vast in every respect. Beyond our prairies filled with wheat, oats, barley, soybeans, corn, and many other familiar cash crops, there are many lesser-known crops—such as lentils, chickpeas, sesame, mustard—exported across the globe to feed our hungry world, and they are converted into different products and sent back home.

Dijon mustard, which I have long used daily, is a perfect example. I had always assumed it was French, but its origin is Canadian: Our mustard seed travels from Canada to France and is transformed and sent back to us in this most delicious format.

When thinking about cultivated crops here on Vancouver Island, I must admit that at one time my mind mostly wandered to vegetable gardens and small hobby farms that bring food to market—and that's about it. I figured that because our land is rocky, and topsoil is basically nonexistent, it would be logical to assume that even though our weather is warm and wet, not much can grow. But the more Danielle and I learned, the more we realized our assumptions were wrong. While it's true that our landscape isn't ideal for large, efficient, cultivated crops when compared to the Fraser Valley, or the Okanagan, or the wide-open prairie farmlands, it's also true that the crops that grow here on the Island are varied and astonishing.

Ancient grain wheat may be the most well-known. Our Red Fife wheat is wholesome and rich, and it makes delicious breads and pastries. It's unadulterated, or crossed, or changed in any way from its original state as wheat. Many artisan bakeries on the Island have their own grain mills and small silos outside, so they can process the grain all on their own. Often the baker is the only one to touch the grain after it leaves the field; the flour is milled on-site and is usually used the day it's milled. This approach allows bakers versatility for when they mill the flour for rich, deep, nutty breads in contrast to more finely milled flour for pastries, croissants, and cakes. This versatility in the process means there is little to no food waste, making the milling process sustainable, and supporting our farmers and local businesses, allowing islanders to enjoy their local crop in its purest form.

Beyond wheat, oats are grown in the central Island, between Port Alberni and Qualicum; here you will also find crops of barley, kamut, spelt, rye, lentils, flax, and more.

Because of our warm, temperate climate, olives grow on the south slopes of the Cowichan Valley. The only olive-oil-producing grove is on Salt Spring Island, the largest of the Gulf Islands surrounding Vancouver Island. In Sidney, a small town just outside Victoria, a farmer cultivates lemons, limes, oranges, kumquats, and other citrus that most would never expect to find in Canada.

Kiwis grow naturally on vines. Green figs and fragrant lavender are cultivated everywhere from backyards to the fields of the Saanich Peninsula. A wide variety of leafy greens bursts forth at almost any time of year, except August when it's scorching hot and dry. Fresh herbs are often used as ground cover under trees in cherry, apple, and pear orchards. The soil, rich with nutrients from the bedrock, moss, falling leaves, pine needles, and other plants create this beautiful ecosystem where almost everything grows and our fields overflow. The innovation, creativity, and purpose with which the farmers and producers on Vancouver Island work never fails to astonish me when I attend farmers markets and seek out all that this Island produces.

Each recipe in this chapter features an ingredient from a Vancouver Island field, whether it's sprouts, leafy greens or rainbow chard, a platter of roasted radishes, hazelnuts in coffee cake swirls, or lavender in sandwich cookies. It's surprising how many different flavours an island field can produce! —EL

field

field

Easy Artisan Seedy Soda Bread

MAKES ONE 9-INCH
ROUND LOAF

4 cups Red Fife flour
2 tsp baking soda
1 tsp fine sea salt
½ cup sunflower seeds
½ cup pumpkin seeds
¼ cup hemp or flax seeds
2¼ cups buttermilk

We are lucky enough to have Red Fife wheat, a complex, protein-rich, ancient heritage grain, grown right here in Metchosin. I always have Red Fife flour on hand, knowing it fills my baking with extra goodness—not to mention its super-tasty, dense, nutty flavour. If you can't get Red Fife, any good whole wheat flour will do for this loaf. —DLA

Preheat the oven to 400°F. Line a baking sheet with parchment paper.

Sift the flour, baking soda, and salt into a large mixing bowl. Add the seeds and stir to distribute them evenly. Pour in the buttermilk and stir to combine. If necessary, add a drop or two more buttermilk until the mixture just comes together to form a soft, slightly sticky dough.

Turn the dough out onto a well-floured work surface, knead it gently for about 1 minute, and then form it into a ball about 6 inches in diameter. Dust generously with flour and, using a sharp knife, score a cross into the top, cutting about ½ inch down into the loaf. Place the bread on the prepared baking sheet and bake for 65–75 minutes, or until a wooden skewer inserted in the centre comes out clean.

Remove from the oven and place the loaf on a cooling rack to keep the crust nice and crispy.

Red Fife Wheat

Red Fife is Canada's oldest variety of wheat, and in the 1860s it was the most popular variety of wheat grown in the country, well-known for being an excellent bread wheat. It is the genetic grandparent to most of the wheat grown in Canada today. Over time, however, new varieties of wheat were introduced, and they became favoured for their resistance to pests or fungus. Red Fife wheat eventually all but disappeared. But in 1988, Sharon Rempel, a heritage seed conservationist and the original creator of "Seedy Saturday," planted seven varieties of historic Canadian wheat, Red Fife among them, as part of her Heritage Wheat Project based in BC.

Since then Red Fife has made a huge comeback, along with several other ancient varieties of wheat and whole grains.

Many people who struggle with gluten intolerance can enjoy Red Fife sourdough bread. Artisan bakers use traditional fermentation (the bread is free from artificial yeasts and preservatives), which make it easily digestible. And because of the natural nutrients found in this grain, the natural yeast has plenty to feast on, and so the flour lends itself well to traditional baking methods.

Due to its unique heirloom status, its nutty and deeply rich flavour, and relatively lower levels of gluten, this wheat is truly unique. As a whole wheat berry, it tastes similar to wild rice. As a whole grain flour, the taste is comparable to rye and spelt: very textured and rich. When husked and finely milled, the flour is soft and fine, similar to a cake and pastry flour, but with a complex flavour.

More and more farmers are growing it, and more artisanal bakers are milling and experimenting with it. You won't come by it easily: It's not readily commercially available, but you will find several places on Vancouver Island that use and supply it, often milling it. In fact, its robust flavour is preserved by milling the flour slowly at low temperatures, using traditional stone milling technology.

To find it, check out Nootka Rose Milling in Metchosin, Fol Epi Organic Bread and Pastry, Wildfire Bakery, and Fry's Bakery in Victoria, BC, and True Grain Bread in Cowichan Bay and Courtenay.

field

field

Overnight Island Oats
with Bumbleberry Compote

Oats

2 cups rolled oats

¼ cup packed brown sugar, plus 2 tsp brown sugar, divided

2 Tbsp ground flax seeds

2 Tbsp chia seeds

1½ tsp ground nutmeg, divided

1 tsp ground allspice

½ tsp ground cinnamon

4 cups milk (almond, soy, or 2%)

Bumbleberry Compote

1 Tbsp cornstarch

2 Tbsp cold water

1 cup frozen forest berries (blackberries, black currants, salal berries, blueberries)

2 Tbsp lemon juice

Wild oats might not be the first thing you think of when you think of Vancouver Island produce, but they grow in the north-central parts of the Island and you'll find them in various markets and stores. These hand-rolled, artisan oats are nuttier than standard grocery store oats and almost perfectly round. Their flakiness and crunchiness makes them perfect for making overnight oats, as they get nice and plump instead of going soggy, and their nuttiness is a perfect complement to the berries. —EL

In a large bowl, mix together the oats, ¼ cup of the sugar, the flax and chia seeds, 1 tsp of the nutmeg, the allspice, and the cinnamon. Place ½ cup of this mixture in each of four 2-cup mason jars or similar sealable glass jars. Add 1 cup of milk to each jar and mix with a spoon to combine. Seal the jars and put in the fridge to soak for at least 12 hours, or up to 3 days.

In a small saucepan, whisk together the remaining 2 tsp sugar, the remaining ½ tsp nutmeg, and the cornstarch with the cold water until the mixture is completely lump-free. Fold in the frozen berries, drizzle the lemon juice overtop, and place over medium heat, covered, to allow the berries to thaw, 2–3 minutes, stirring once or twice.

Remove the lid and increase the heat to medium-high. Watch the berries carefully, stirring occasionally, as they come to a boil. Boil for 1 minute then remove from the heat.

Serve immediately or allow to cool. This will keep in an airtight container in the fridge for up to 3 months.

To serve, remove the lid from the jar of oats and top with a dollop of compote. A dollop of yogurt is also tasty.

field

Blueberry Lemon Thyme Breakfast Waffles

SERVES 4

Blueberry Lemon Thyme
  Syrup
2 cups fresh blueberries
4 sprigs lemon thyme
¼ cup granulated sugar
2 Tbsp cornstarch
½ cup water

Waffles
4 eggs, separated
2½ cups milk (2% or
  whole)
¾ cup salted butter, melted
2 cups all-purpose flour
¼ cup granulated sugar
2 tsp baking powder
Whipped cream,
  for serving

Time-consuming? Yes. Many components? Yes. Worth the trouble? Definitely. When blueberries come into season, these are one of the first things on the menu at my house, and we all crave them for weeks afterwards. To get the crispiness on the outside and the light-as-air texture on the inside, fold the whipped egg whites very gently into the batter. (Note: You'll need a waffle iron for this recipe.) —EL

To make the syrup, rinse and stem the berries. Place them in a small saucepan and add the thyme. In a small bowl, whisk together the sugar and cornstarch until no lumps remain, pour in the water, and whisk until thick. Pour this over the berries and place the pan over medium heat. Bring to a rolling boil for 1 minute, stirring constantly, then remove from the heat. Allow to cool to almost room temperature, then discard the thyme.

To make the waffles, using a stand mixer fitted with the whisk attachment, whip the egg whites to soft peaks. Set aside.

In a large measuring jug, whisk together the milk and butter. Whisk in the egg yolks in a single addition. In a mixing bowl, whisk together the flour, sugar, and baking powder. Make a well in the centre of the dry ingredients, pour in the milk mixture, and whisk to form a thick batter. Gently fold in the egg whites to combine. The batter will be slightly lumpy.

Follow the instructions for your waffle iron. You want the waffles to be a deep golden brown.

Serve the waffles fresh from the iron with a dollop of whipped cream and a spoonful of blueberry lemon thyme syrup.

The waffle batter will keep in an airtight container in the fridge for up to 2 days. It's best if you use it straight from the fridge, rather than letting it come to room temperature. If it separates, give it a few good folds with a spatula before using it. The syrup will keep in an airtight container in the fridge for up to 2 weeks.

field

Red Fife Honey Scones
with Strawberry Butter

MAKES NINE 3-INCH
SCONES

Scones
3 cups Red Fife flour
2 heaping teaspoons
　　baking powder
¼ cup granulated sugar
½ cup unsalted butter,
　　chilled but not hard
1¼ cups buttermilk
1 egg, whisked

Strawberry butter
1 cup unsalted butter,
　　room temperature
¼ cup pure maple syrup
1 tsp pink peppercorns
4–5 strawberries, washed,
　　dried, and diced

Red Fife wheat is the key to the earthy robust and nutty flavour of these scones (for more on Red Fife wheat, see page 33). They are less "biscuit" and more "soda bread" in texture (although still flaky), and the nuttiness of the scone offsets the naturally sweet strawberry butter. The perfect addition to a summer afternoon tea after picking up a pint of local strawberries from the market. —EL

Preheat the oven to 400°F. Line a baking sheet with parchment paper.

To make the scones, in a medium-size bowl, whisk together the flour and baking powder. Using a pastry blender or two knives, cut in the butter until the mixture resembles coarse oatmeal. Make a well in the flour mixture and pour in the buttermilk and egg. Using a wooden spoon or spatula, mix together until fully combined, scraping up any dry bits from the bottom of the bowl. You will have a soft dough.

Turn the dough out onto a well-floured work surface and roll into a large disc about 1 inch thick. Using a large glass or cookie cutter, cut 3-inch diameter circles in the dough. Transfer to the prepared baking sheet and bake for 12–15 minutes.

While the scones are baking, prepare the butter. Place the butter in a bowl and, using hand-held beaters, beat it until it's very soft and fluffy and almost doubled in volume, 3–4 minutes. Scrape down the bowl, pour in the maple syrup, and beat until combined. Gently crush the pink peppercorns, add them to the butter, and beat well. You'll see specks of peppercorns evenly distributed throughout. Ensure the strawberries are very dry and then add them to the mixture. Beat on low speed until fully and evenly incorporated. The butter will be soft, fluffy, and beautifully pink, with some pieces of strawberries showing through.

Remove the scones from the oven, transfer to a wire rack, and let cool for 3–5 minutes, just until cool enough to handle but still warm. Place on a serving platter and serve with strawberry butter on the side.

The scones will keep in an airtight container in the fridge for up to 4 days. The butter will keep in an airtight container in the fridge for up to 3 days or in the freezer for up to 1 month.

Roasted Radishes
with Honey Butter

SERVES 4–6

1 lb fresh radishes

1 Tbsp extra virgin olive oil

2 Tbsp unsalted butter

2 tsp honey, preferably
clover or other fragrant
variety

Flaked sea salt

Not just for salads, radishes really shine as a roasted vegetable in the summer months when the farmers markets are overflowing with a huge assortment of varietals. They have a deeply savoury flavour that pairs well with the sweet fragrance of a honey butter—perfect alongside grilled steaks or other strongly flavoured meat. —DLA

Preheat the oven to 425°F. Line a rimmed baking sheet with parchment paper.

Slice the radishes in half lengthwise and trim the green tops down to about 1 inch long. Retain the leaves and wash away any sand. Toss the radishes and leaves in the oil and place on the prepared baking sheet. Bake for 5 minutes. Remove the radishes from the oven. Leave the oven switched on.

Toss the radishes with the butter and honey until the butter has melted and the radishes are well coated. Return to the oven and bake for another 10 minutes, or until just crispy on the outside and tender on the inside. Add sea salt to taste. Serve immediately or hold in a warming oven for up to 30 minutes.

field

Quick Summer Farm Pickles

MAKES 2 CUPS

1½ cups vinegar
   (scc chart)
1 Tbsp granulated sugar
1 tsp fine sea salt
1 Tbsp minced shallot
2 cups fruit or vegetables
   (see chart)

My dear friend Angie is, in my opinion, the undisputed pickle queen, and she taught me just about everything I know about preserving. The glory of this particular recipe of hers is that you can use it with just about every vegetable or fruit you can think of, there's no canning required, and it's ready to pop on the table in 30 minutes. A perfect way to use up the glut of fresh veg that flows in from the fields in the summer. I've included a chart that shows some of my favourite fruit/veg and vinegar combinations, plus their sitting times. —DLA

Place the vinegar in a medium bowl. Add the sugar and salt, and stir to dissolve. Add the shallot along with the fruit or vegetables and let sit, uncovered, at room temperature for 10–30 minutes, depending on how soft you want your pickles to be. Drain the pickles from the pickling solution and serve. These can be eaten the day you make them or you can keep them in an airtight container in the fridge for up to 2 weeks.

Fruit/ veg*	vinegar	sitting time
Raspberries	red wine vinegar	10 minutes
Blueberries	red wine vinegar	10 minutes
Cucumbers (English or regular are fine)	white wine vinegar	15 minutes
Green beans	apple cider vinegar	20 minutes
Beets	white wine vinegar	25 minutes
Carrots	apple cider vinegar	30 minutes
Radishes	apple cider vinegar	25 minutes
Turnips	white wine vinegar	30 minutes

*Berries can be left whole, green beans can be trimmed but otherwise left whole, and any particularly crunchy vegetables, such as carrots or radishes, should be sliced quite thinly.

Butter-Roasted Delicata

SERVES 4

1 large or 2 small (2–3 lb in
    total) delicata squash
¼ cup salted butter
2 Tbsp pure maple syrup
2 Tbsp orange juice
2 Tbsp chopped rosemary
    leaves

Move over, butternut! Delicata is in the house. This tasty, oh-so-sweet, and beautiful squash is not something to be trifled with! Being slender and long with a soft skin, it's perfect to cut into spears to roast in an herb citrus butter. This simple side is perfect with Cedar-Grilled Spatchcock Herb-Rubbed Chicken (page 125) or Ortega-Braised Chicken with Wild Morels (page 184). —EL

Preheat the oven to 400°F. Line a rimmed baking sheet with parchment paper.

Using a sharp knife, slice the squash in half lengthwise. Using a teaspoon, scrape out and discard the seeds. Lay the squash cut side down and cut it into 1-inch-thick slices. Spread the slices in a single layer on the prepared baking sheet.

In a small saucepan over low heat, melt the butter, and then whisk in the maple syrup and orange juice until fully emulsified. Brush this mixture over the squash slices, then flip them over and brush the other side, ensuring they are well coated. Drizzle any remaining butter mixture overtop. Sprinkle with the rosemary.

Roast for 35 minutes, until fork-tender and caramelized on the outside. Remove from the oven and allow to cool slightly before serving.

The cooked squash will keep in an airtight container in the fridge for up to 1 week.

Roasted Garlic and Honeyed Chèvre Dip

MAKES 1 CUP

1 large bulb garlic
1 Tbsp extra virgin olive oil
1 cup fresh goat cheese
2 Tbsp fragrant, runny
    honey
6 fresh basil leaves, torn
    into small pieces
Flaked sea salt

We are blessed here on the Gulf Islands to have the perfect soil for growing incredibly tasty garlic. This recipe from my dear friend Angie is one of my favourite ways to enjoy the sweetly pungent magical transformation that comes when you roast a whole bulb and mix it with the freshest possible goat cheese and a good, local honey. —DLA

Preheat the oven to 375°F.

Remove the papery outside layer of the garlic. Cut about ¼ inch from the top of the bulb to expose the cloves. Drizzle the oil over the exposed cloves. Wrap the bulb in two layers of aluminum foil and place on a rimmed baking sheet. Bake for 30–40 minutes, or until the garlic cloves are soft and a deep caramel colour. Let cool slightly and remove the cloves from the bulb husk.

Squeeze the roasted garlic cloves into a food processor, add the goat cheese, honey, basil, and a pinch of salt, and pulse to combine. Serve with baguette, crisps, crackers, or a crudité platter.

This will keep in an airtight container in the fridge for up to 5 days.

Roasted Brussels Sprouts
with Crispy Bacon and Yellow Point Cranberries

SERVES 4–6

½ lb slab bacon, cut into
　½-inch cubes
1 lb Brussels sprouts,
　halved
1 cup fresh cranberries
2 Tbsp pure maple syrup
1 tsp chili flakes (optional)
Flaked sea salt and ground
　black pepper

Those who claim they don't like Brussels sprouts simply haven't had them cooked like this. In this recipe, these Island-grown sprouts, picked at the height of their flavour in our first frosty days of autumn, are cooked to a savoury and deeply satisfying crisp with a sweet-sour edge, courtesy of our gorgeous, locally grown Yellow Point cranberries. I also like to spice them up with some chili flakes for a bit of an extra zing. —DLA

Preheat the oven to 375°F. Line a 13- × 9-inch baking dish with parchment paper.

Place the bacon in the baking dish in a single layer. Bake for 15 minutes, or until the fat starts to render out. Add the Brussels sprouts and toss to coat completely in the fat. Bake for another 10 minutes, just until the sprouts begin to crisp, and then add the cranberries.

Turn up the oven temperature to 400°F.

Bake for another 3–5 minutes, just until the cranberries begin to sizzle and pop. The bacon and Brussels sprouts should be good and crispy. Add the maple syrup and chili flakes (if using) and toss lightly to combine. Season with a pinch of salt and pepper to taste. Serve immediately.

field

Heirloom Tomato and Goat Cheese Platter
with Candied Jalapeños

SERVES 4

4 large tomatoes,
    preferably in contrasting
    colours
½ cup goat cheese,
    crumbled
½ cup candied jalapeños
2 Tbsp balsamic vinegar
2 Tbsp extra virgin olive oil
½ tsp flaked sea salt

This salad is as beautiful as it is delicious, and it screams summer. When I'm hunting down heirloom tomatoes at my local farmers market, this is the recipe that's on my mind. Heirloom tomatoes are traditional ancient varieties, which means they are bursting with flavour when compared to hothouse or grocery store varieties. Look for different shapes and colours to make this salad as beautiful as it is flavourful. —EL

Slice the tomatoes and arrange them on a platter. Scatter the goat cheese and jalapeños over the tomatoes, leaving the jalapeños intact in case guests don't like the pop of heat. Drizzle the balsamic and oil overtop, sprinkle with the salt, and serve immediately.

This is best eaten the day you make it, but you can store leftovers in an airtight container in the fridge overnight.

Garden Herb Green Goddess Dressing

MAKES 1 CUP

¼ cup chopped parsley
   (curly or flat-leaf)
5 sprigs of tarragon
4 basil leaves
¼ cup water
1 clove garlic
½ cup Greek yogurt
¼ cup mayonnaise
Flaked sea salt and ground
   black pepper
2 tsp finely chopped chives

This dressing is delicious with almost anything, so keep some in the fridge at all times! My favourite way to use it is to pour some over fresh tomatoes and creamy mozzarella cheese. The vibrancy of fresh herbs makes all the ingredients feel alive—and if you have access to fresh herbs all year around, know that this dressing feels even more special in the winter months. —EL

Place the parsley, tarragon, and basil in a blender, add water, and blend until the herbs are a smooth liquid. Smash the clove of garlic, add it to the blender, and pulse to fully combine. Place the yogurt and mayo in a bowl, stir to combine, pour the herb mixture overtop, and mix into a thick dressing. Garnish with chopped chives.

This will keep in an airtight container in the fridge for up to 1 week.

field

Summer Bounty Veggie Platter
with Herby Yogurt Dip

MAKES 2 CUPS

Blanched Vegetables
baby carrots
asparagus
sugar snap peas
broccoli
broccolini

*Roasted or Grilled and
    Cooled Vegetables*
roasted peppers
radishes
cauliflower
eggplant
baby turnips
radicchio

Raw Vegetables
cucumbers
tomatoes
lettuce

Dip
2 cups Greek yogurt
2 cups finely chopped,
    mixed fresh garden
    herbs (mint, basil,
    tarragon, flat-leaf
    parsley)
½ cup crumbled
    feta cheese

Much like the Ferryman's Lunch Platter (page 118), this is more of a suggestion than a recipe, and the assortment of vegetables you choose should reflect whatever is currently fresh and available. There are no real rules here, but diversity is key. Some vegetables become even sweeter when blanched; others are delicious if roasted then chilled. I've listed some of my favourite options, but the real key to success here is simply using fresh produce. —DLA

Mix all of the dip ingredients together. Refrigerate until ready to serve. The dip will keep in an airtight container in the fridge for up to 5 days.

field

Radish and Sprout Salad
with Grilled Lemon Vinaigrette

SERVES 8–10

Salad
6–8 assorted radishes, washed well and trimmed
1 cup micro sprouts, such as broccoli or pea
Ground black pepper

Vinaigrette
2 lemons, cut in half lengthwise
2 Tbsp plus 2 tsp extra virgin olive oil, divided
1 tsp Dijon mustard
1 tsp honey
Fine sea salt

The assortment of radishes that are grown here on the Island is truly staggering—and that variety is one of the things that makes this salad so truly beautiful, not to mention delicious. It's a great addition to any barbecue menu and goes really well with grilled Comox Valley porterhouse steaks (pg 140). —DLA

Using a mandoline, slice the radishes very, very thinly. They should be almost transparent. Cover with plastic wrap in the fridge for up to 3-4 hours if you're not serving them immediately.

To make the vinaigrette, you can either use a barbecue grill, a cast iron grill pan, or the broil setting on your oven. Brush the cut sides of the lemons with the 2 tsp of oil and grill or broil, cut side up, for 3–5 minutes, or until they're slightly charred. Remove from the heat and let cool completely.

Squeeze the juice from the cooled lemons into a mason jar, add the remaining 2 Tbsp oil, the Dijon, and honey. Put the lid on the jar and shake well to combine. Season to taste with salt.

When you're ready to serve, scatter the sliced radishes onto a serving platter. Sprinkle the sprouts overtop and drizzle with the vinaigrette. Season with pepper to taste.

This is best eaten the day you make it. The vinaigrette will keep in an airtight container in the fridge for up to 3 days.

field

Island Greens Salad

with Sparkling Vinaigrette

SERVES 4

¼ cup mild extra virgin
   olive oil
3 Tbsp sparkling wine
2 tsp grainy Dijon mustard
1 tsp shallots, sliced
¼ tsp coarse sea salt
6 cups torn lettuce leaves
   (leaf or Boston are my
   favourite for this)

Using a sparkling wine in a vinaigrette may seem strange, but the effervescence makes for a delightfully light dressing. I use Charme De L'Ile from Unsworth Vineyards in the Cowichan Valley and a mild olive oil, which pulls the fruity notes out of the wine. This a perfect use for the end of a bottle of wine, and guests will ask for your secret ingredient. —EL

In a small bowl, whisk together the oil, wine, Dijon, shallots, and salt. Place the lettuce in a serving bowl and drizzle with the dressing. Using your hands, gently massage the dressing into the lettuce leaves. Serve immediately.

This is best eaten the day you make it. The vinaigrette will keep in an airtight container in the fridge for up to 3 days.

field

Butternut Squash, Kale, and Cranberry Salad

SERVES 6

Salad

1 cup red quinoa

1 lb butternut squash,
   peeled, seeds discarded,
   and cubed

2 Tbsp extra virgin olive oil

Flaked sea salt

1 large bunch curly kale
   (green or red)

1 cup dried cranberries

Dressing

¼ cup extra virgin olive oil

3 Tbsp apple cider vinegar

2 Tbsp tahini

1 tsp chipotle chili powder
   (optional)

Fine sea salt and cracked
   black pepper

This is one of my favourite harvest salads, and it's a guaranteed crowd-pleaser for any autumnal gathering. It makes a particularly good vegetarian buffet option and the recipe can be easily doubled or tripled to feed a larger group. —DLA

To make the salad, cook the quinoa according to the package instructions. Once it's cooked, fluff with a fork, then set aside to let cool. Put quinoa in a serving bowl.

Preheat the oven to 400°F. Line a rimmed baking sheet with parchment paper.

In a medium bowl, toss the squash with the oil and a pinch of salt. Lay the squash out in a single layer on the prepared baking sheet and bake for 7–8 minutes. Flip the squash over and roast for another 5–6 minutes. Continue to flip to cook all of the sides until golden and slightly crispy. Remove from the heat and set aside.

Wash and dry the kale, discard the tough central stalks, and tear the leaves into bite-sized pieces.

To make the dressing, in a small bowl, whisk together the oil, vinegar, tahini, chili powder (if using), and a pinch of salt and pepper.

Add the cooled squash, kale, and cranberries to the quinoa and pour the dressing overtop. Toss to combine at least 20 minutes before serving to allow the flavours to meld. The dressed salad can be stored in an airtight container in the fridge for up to 5 days.

Deep-Fried Zucchini Blossoms
with Ricotta, Mint, and Sugar Snap Pea Filling

MAKES 12 (SERVES 4–6)

3 oz ricotta cheese
(see page 116 for how
to make homemade
ricotta)

¾ cup freshly shelled
sugar snap peas

½ cup finely chopped mint
leaves

2 tsp lemon juice

Grated zest of 1 lemon

Fine sea salt and ground
black pepper

12 zucchini blossoms,
rinsed, dried, stamens
removed

1 cup rice or chickpea flour

1 cup sparkling water

Vegetable oil, for frying

I have always loved eating stuffed zucchini blossoms but was daunted by their delicacy when it came to cooking them. Turns out they're not as fragile as I thought, and actually really easy to work with. I make them all the time now with a variety of fillings, but this one is definitely my favourite. You can easily find the blossoms at your local farmers markets in the summer. If you've planted any squash or pumpkin in your own garden, pinching off a few blossoms in early summer shouldn't harm your crop at all. —DLA

In a large mixing bowl, mix the ricotta with the peas, mint, lemon juice and zest, and a pinch of salt and pepper. Spoon a heaping tablespoon of filling into each blossom. Close the blossoms and gently twist the petals to seal.

In a separate bowl, whisk together the flour and sparkling water to make a smooth batter.

Line a large plate with paper towels.

In a large, heavy-bottomed saucepan or Dutch oven-style pot, over medium heat, pour in enough oil to fill the pan about a third of the way up. When a deep-fry thermometer inserted into the oil shows 365°F, dip the stuffed blossoms into the batter and allow any excess to drip off. Fry the blossoms in batches of three for 2–3 minutes, turning occasionally, until golden brown. Once cooked, remove the blossoms from the oil with a slotted spoon and place on the prepared plate to drain off any excess oil.

Serve immediately or keep warm and crispy in an oven set to 200°F for up to 30 minutes.

field

Rainbow Chard and Roasted Yam Grain Bowl

SERVES 4

Garlic yogurt sauce

1 cup Greek yogurt

¼ cup lime juice (2–3 limes)

2 cloves garlic, minced

½ tsp ground ginger

½ tsp fine sea salt

½ tsp ground black pepper

Grain bowl

1½ cups dried spelt berries

3 cups chicken or vegetable stock

2 small yams

4 Tbsp extra virgin olive oil, divided

2 Tbsp lime juice, divided

1 tsp ground cumin

1½ cups cherry tomatoes

1 tsp fine sea salt

1 tsp ground black pepper

½ tsp chopped rosemary leaves

4 stems and leaves of rainbow Swiss chard

4 radishes

This is a hearty dish that's perfect in both winter, for a simple, cozy meal, and summer, for a filling, yet fresh meal. When you massage olive oil and lime juice into chard, it keeps the flavour fresh and bright. The radish and spelt berries both add richness to the texture of this dish. I like to use spelt grown in the central-northern parts of Vancouver Island. Farro or pearl barley are also tasty choices, and for a gluten-free option, replace the grain with quinoa. Keep a close eye on timing so that everything is still warm when you serve this. —EL

To make the garlic yogurt sauce, whisk together all the ingredients in a mixing bowl and refrigerate, uncovered, until ready to serve.

To make the grain bowl, rinse the spelt berries and place them in a saucepan with the stock. Bring to a rolling boil, uncovered, over medium-high heat. Turn down the heat to low, cover the pan with a lid, and simmer, covered, for 30–40 minutes, until the spelt berries are tender and soft but still meaty in texture.

Preheat the oven to 425°F. Line a rimmed baking sheet with parchment paper.

Peel the yams and cut them into ½-inch cubes. Place them in a medium bowl and drizzle with 2 Tbsp of the oil, 5 tsp of the lime juice, and the cumin. Toss to coat well and then place on the prepared baking sheet. Place the tomatoes in a small bowl, drizzle them with 1 Tbsp of the oil, roll them around to coat them evenly, and add to the yams. Sprinkle the salt, pepper, and rosemary overtop.

Roast for 20 minutes, turn the yams and tomatoes so they brown evenly, and roast for another 15 minutes.

Chop the Swiss chard stems into small dice and slice the leaves into ribbons. Transfer to a medium bowl, drizzle with the remaining 1 Tbsp oil and 1 tsp lime juice, and massage well. Set aside. Thinly slice radishes and place them in a bowl of cold water to crisp up their texture and mellow their flavour.

Divide the spelt berries evenly between four bowls, top with yams, tomatoes, chard, and radishes, and dollop the garlic yogurt sauce on the side. Serve immediately and enjoy!

The salad is best eaten the day it's made. The sauce will keep in an airtight container in the fridge for up to 3 days.

field

Sweet Corn and Bacon Chowder

SERVES 4–6

6 slices thick-cut bacon

1 cup diced cooking onion

1 medium red bell pepper, diced

2 cloves garlic, minced

1 tsp chili powder

6 cups fresh corn kernels (cut from about 12 ears), divided

6 cups chicken stock, divided

4 medium yellow potatoes, peeled and diced

Coarse sea salt and ground black pepper

Pinch of paprika

This is one of my favourite ways to use the glut of corn that comes in at the end of harvest. It's also free of dairy (a plus in our dairy-sensitive house), and cuts out a lot of the fat that traditional chowders contain. If you like your food a little spicy, a pinch of chipotle pepper is a nice addition, but don't feel you have to add it. I love to use Hertel's nitrate free bacon from Port Alberni, but any good quality, thick-cut rashers will do. —DLA

In a large Dutch oven or soup pot over medium-high heat, cook the bacon until crispy. Remove the bacon from the pan and set aside. Turn down the heat to medium and add the onion and bell pepper to the bacon drippings. Sauté for 2–3 minutes, just until the onion starts to soften. Add the garlic and chili powder and sauté, stirring constantly, for 1 more minute. Add 3 cups of the corn kernels and cook for another 3–4 minutes, or just until the kernels begin to soften and turn a deep yellow colour. Add 3 cups of the stock and the potatoes and bring the soup to a low rolling boil.

In the meantime, place the remaining 3 cups of corn kernels and 3 cups of chicken stock in a blender and purée on high speed until smooth. Add the puréed mixture to the soup pot and heat through until the potatoes are soft. Season with salt and pepper to taste, and sprinkle top with a pinch of paprika.

field

Red Fife Flatbread Three Ways

SERVES 4

2 cups Red Fife flour

1 cup all-purpose flour,
   plus more for dusting

1 tsp baking powder

1 tsp fine sea salt

2 Tbsp honey

1 Tbsp quick-rise yeast

1 cup warm water (hand-
   hot is fine)

⅓ cup extra virgin olive oil,
   plus more for the bowl

Red Fife is so nutty and rich that I find I really love working with it. (See page 33 for more about this wonderful ingredient.) It's intriguing, too, that whole-grain flours in yeasted dough don't need to be kneaded as much as white flour does. The coarseness of the grain does some of the legwork for you. If you don't have Red Fife flour on hand, use stone-ground whole wheat flour instead. —EL

Sift both flours, the baking powder, and salt together into a large mixing bowl.

Place the honey and yeast in a small liquid measure and add the water. Let sit until the yeast begins to froth, about 5 minutes.

Preheat the oven to 200°F and then switch it off without opening the door.

Make a well in the flour mixture and pour in the frothy yeast mixture, followed by the oil. Using a wooden spoon or spatula, mix until the dough is pulling away from the sides of the bowl and the mixture is fully incorporated. Turn onto a well-floured work surface and knead for 8 minutes, until the dough is smooth and elastic. Shape the dough into a ball, place in an oiled bowl, and turn to coat completely. Cover with a tea towel and place in the warm oven for 15–20 minutes, until almost doubled in bulk. Punch down the dough and turn it onto a well-floured work surface again. Knead it once or twice, divide it in half, and roll each half into a ball. (At this point, you can freeze the dough. Place each ball in a resealable plastic bag or freezer container for up to 3 months. Let it thaw completely in the fridge before using.)

Preheat the oven to 450°F. Lightly flour two baking sheets (any type of flour is fine for this).

Place the dough balls on a well-floured work surface, cover with a dry tea towel, and let rise for 8–10 minutes. The dough will look soft and puffy. Flatten each ball of dough into a 12 to 14-inch diameter disc with your hands or a rolling pin. Place each disc on a floured baking sheet. Add the toppings of your choice (or bake it plain!) and bake for 8–10 minutes (without a topping), or 10–12 minutes with a topping, until puffed and golden. I usually bake one flatbread at a time for best results.

Flatbread will keep in an airtight container in the fridge for up to 3 days, although topped flatbread is definitely best the day it's made.

Each of the toppings listed on page 73 makes enough for two flatbreads. Simply mix together all the ingredients and sprinkle overtop the flatbreads. Delicious!

Caramelized Onions, Toasted Hazelnuts, and Blue Cheese

I like to use Bleu Claire cheese from Little Qualicum Cheeseworks for this. It's a little bit firm but it crumbles easily.

1 cup caramelized onions
¼ cup extra virgin olive oil
1 tsp coarse sea salt
½ cup whole hazelnuts
½ cup crumbled blue cheese

Roasted Pear, Pancetta, Chèvre, and Sage

1 Bartlett pear, peeled and sliced
9 slices pancetta
½ cup chèvre
6–8 sage leaves, torn

Leek, Wild Mushrooms, and Ricotta

1 leek
1 cup sliced wild mushrooms
   (shiitake, oyster, chanterelle)
¾ cup ricotta cheese (see page 116 for how
   to make homemade ricotta)
2 Tbsp honey
1 tsp coarse sea salt
2 tsp thyme leaves

field

Roasted Sour Cherry Galette

SERVES 6

Pastry

1½ cups all-purpose flour

½ tsp baking powder

½ tsp fine sea salt

2 Tbsp granulated sugar

⅓ cup salted butter, chilled
   but not hard, cubed

1 egg

2 tsp lemon juice

2 Tbsps cold water

Filling

½ cup plus 2 Tbsp
   granulated sugar

1 vanilla bean

¼ cup cornstarch

3 cups freshly pitted sour
   cherries

2 Tbsp extra virgin olive oil

Sour cherries bring back wonderful memories of my childhood, when my family and I would go to a U-pick cherry orchard—complete with its own massive cherry pitter. Not only was it a time-saver, it was also an endless source of fascination for me. U-pick cherry orchards are less common these days, but I love Silver Rill Berry Farm in Saanichton, and I like to stock up at local farmers markets in July. —EL

To make the pastry, place the flour, baking powder, and salt in a large mixing bowl. Whisk in the sugar to combine, then add the butter. Using a pastry blender or two knives, cut in the butter until the mixture resembles coarse oatmeal. Using a fork, whisk the egg and lemon juice together in a large measuring cup. Add cold water, whisk a little more to fully incorporate, and pour over the flour mixture. Mix the wet and dry ingredients gently together with a wooden spoon, then, using your hands, blend the dough by folding and pressing the pastry into the bowl. Be careful not to overmix. When the pastry just comes together into a ball, wrap it in plastic wrap and refrigerate for at least 30 minutes, or up to overnight.

To make the filling, place the ½ cup sugar in a mixing bowl. Split the vanilla bean in half and scrape the seeds into the sugar. Mix well, until the bean's seeds are evenly distributed and no lumps remain. I prefer to do this with my fingers. Gently whisk in the cornstarch, making sure the mixture is lump-free. Add the cherries and their juices, and toss to coat evenly.

Preheat the oven to 425°F. Line a baking sheet with parchment paper.

Remove the pastry from the fridge and roll it into a 14-inch round shape on a well-floured work surface. Roll up the pastry on the rolling pin and transfer it to the prepared baking sheet. Roll up the edges of the pastry and crimp them to form a lip around the outside. You're aiming for a rustic circle with a crust high enough so that the cherries won't fall out, about 12 inches in diameter, when you're ready for the cherries.

Spoon the cherries into the centre of the pastry and spread them out evenly, making sure the crust is holding them in.

Bake for 15 minutes, then turn down the oven to 350°F without opening the door. Bake for 20 minutes longer. Switch on the broiler to high.

Open the oven door and pull the tart out slightly. Sprinkle with the remaining 2 Tbsp sugar and return to the oven. Broil for 2 minutes, watching carefully, to let the cherries roast and caramelize. Remove galette from the oven and allow to cool completely on the baking sheet before serving.

Hazelnut Caramel Coffee Cake Swirls

MAKES ONE DOZEN
SWIRLS

Dough

3 cups all-purpose flour
2 Tbsp baking powder
¼ cup granulated sugar
½ tsp fine sea salt
¾ cup unsalted butter,
    room temperature,
    cubed
1 egg
1 cup whole milk

Filling

1 cup packed brown sugar
¾ cup crushed hazelnuts
½ cup unsalted butter,
    room temperature
1 tsp ground nutmeg
½ tsp ground cinnamon

Caramel topping

½ cup granulated sugar
2 Tbsp whipping (35%)
    cream

I developed this recipe to combine two of my favourite treats: scones and coffee cake. Here the crumbled coffee cake topping is tucked inside the scone dough. Use local hazelnuts when they're in season in early autumn—their flavour is so buttery and rich. I don't roast them, and I actually leave the skins on for extra flavour and texture. You can remove the skins if you prefer, of course. And be sure to use a wooden spoon where specified. The heat from the caramel will transfer to a metal spoon—which will be no fun for your fingers! —EL

Preheat the oven to 400°F. Place a rack in the centre of the oven. Line a baking sheet with parchment paper.

To make the dough, in a large mixing bowl, whisk the flour and baking powder with the sugar and salt. Using two knives or a pastry blender, cut in the butter until the mixture resembles coarse oatmeal. Make a well in the centre of the dry ingredients and add the egg and milk. Gently mix everything together to form a soft dough.

Place the dough on a well-floured work surface and sprinkle with a little more flour. Roll into a 12- × 8-inch rectangle.

To make the filling, mix together the sugar and hazelnuts. Using a wooden spoon or two knives, cut in the butter, the nutmeg, and cinnamon, mixing well to incorporate. The mixture will be soft and clumpy, with bits of all the ingredients visible.

Spread the filling over the dough, leaving about ½ inch of space all the way around. Gently lift up one long edge of the dough and fold it over the first ½ inch of topping. Now roll the dough up tightly to form a long log. Gently pinch the side seam into the dough and roll the log so it's seam side down. Using a serrated knife, cut the log into 12 evenly sized slices. Place each swirl on the baking sheet, leaving 2–3 inches between each one, as they'll spread quite a bit as they bake. Bake for 15 minutes.

Meanwhile, make the caramel topping. In a small saucepan over medium heat, melt the sugar. Just let it sit and melt, but watch it closely, as it can burn quickly. When the sugar is a deep golden colour and smells deliciously nutty, remove it from the heat, gently pour in the cream, and then, using a wooden spoon, mix well. Allow to cool slightly.

Take the swirls out of the oven, remove from the baking sheet, and place on a wire rack to cool. Drizzle the swirls generously with the caramel, and let them cool a little before enjoying with a warm cup of coffee.

The swirls will keep in an airtight container for up to 4 days on the counter—although I wish you luck with that, as the longest these have ever lasted in my house is about 45 minutes!

field

Shortbread Sandwiches
with Lavender Chèvre Buttercream

MAKES 2 DOZEN
SANDWICH COOKIES

Buttercream
1 cup chèvre
4 cups icing sugar
2 Tbsp whipping (35%)
  cream
Fine sea salt
2 Tbsp fresh lavender
  blossoms

Shortbread
2 cups unsalted butter,
  softened
4 cups all-purpose flour
1 cup icing sugar
1 cup cornstarch
Fine sea salt

These pretty little sandwich cookies are a nod to the long-standing relationship Victoria has with the British afternoon tea tradition. The shortbread is delicious on its own, but I am addicted to the fresh chèvre buttercream that takes them from a regular cookie to a special occasion treat. Fresh lavender blossoms are readily available from lavender farms here on Vancouver Island as well as at farmers markets, but dried culinary lavender will work as well. —DLA

Preheat the oven to 350°F.

To make the buttercream, in a stand mixer fitted with the paddle attachment, beat the chèvre on medium speed until smooth. Add the icing sugar and mix on low speed for a minute or two. Increase the speed to medium and continue mixing for another 1–2 minutes, until well combined and smooth.

Add the cream and a pinch of salt. Mix on medium-high speed for another minute or so, just until everything is well combined and smooth. Scrape down the sides of the bowl and add the lavender blossoms. Using a wooden spoon or spatula, gently fold them in to incorporate.

To make the shortbread, in a stand mixer fitted with the paddle attachment, beat the butter until soft and creamy. In a separate mixing bowl, sift together the flour, icing sugar, cornstarch, and a pinch of salt. Gradually add the dried ingredients to the creamed butter, mixing just enough to incorporate them into a cohesive dough.

Turn the dough out onto a lightly floured work surface and knead until the mixture begins to crack slightly, 3–4 minutes. Roll out to a disc about ⅓-inch thick. Cut out the cookies with a 2-inch round cookie cutter and place at least 1 inch apart on an ungreased baking sheet. (Remember, you need an even number of cookies to make the sandwiches.)

Bake for 10–12 minutes, just until the edges begin to brown. Let cool on the baking sheet until firm.

To assemble, spread 1 Tbsp of buttercream on a cookie and top with another to create a sandwich.

Any unused buttercream will keep in an airtight container in the fridge for up to 7 days. Unassembled cookies will keep in an airtight container at room temperature for up to 2 weeks.

Strawberry Rhubarb Crumble Pie

MAKES ONE 9-INCH PIE

1 cup packed brown sugar

¾ cup all-purpose flour

¾ tsp ground nutmeg, divided

½ tsp ground allspice

½ cup cold salted butter, cubed

4 cups chopped rhubarb

3 cups chopped strawberries

1 cup granulated sugar

⅓ cup cornstarch

½ tsp fine sea salt

1 batch chilled galette pastry (page 74)

1 Tbsp lemon juice

Rhubarb starts to make itself known in the early spring, when gardens on Vancouver Island are just coming alive and whispering to us that summer is almost here and CSA boxes will soon be spilling over with fresh fruits and vegetables. Rhubarb and strawberry make the perfect duo if you're looking for sweet and tart. And a pinch of nutmeg and allspice adds just the right amount of spice. —EL

Preheat the oven to 425°F. Place the oven rack on the bottom third of the oven. Line a rimmed baking sheet with parchment paper.

In a small bowl, place the brown sugar, flour, ½ tsp of the nutmeg, and the allspice. Stir to combine and add the butter. Using a pastry blender or two knives, mix everything together to form a soft crumble. Set aside.

Place the rhubarb and strawberries in a large bowl. Sprinkle with the granulated sugar, cornstarch, salt, and remaining ¼ tsp of nutmeg (in that order) and toss well to combine.

Roll out the prepared pastry to a 10-inch circle. Carefully transfer to a 9-inch pie plate. Press down gently and crimp the pastry edges. Pour in the fruit and drizzle with the lemon juice. Sprinkle the crumble generously over the pie, pressing it gently over the fruit.

Place the pie plate on the prepared baking sheet. Bake for 15 minutes, turn down the oven to 325°F without opening the door. Bake for 45 minutes, until the pastry is golden and the fruit is bubbling under and through the crumble.

Remove from the oven and allow to cool at least 6 hours or overnight. If the pie is cut before it is fully set, the fruit will ooze everywhere. While that is tasty, it makes it hard to cut the pie and store the leftovers.

The pie will keep, covered with a tea towel, at room temperature for 3 days, or in an airtight container in the fridge for up to 1 week.

field

Rhubarb Skillet Cake

6 Tbsp unsalted butter,
 melted, plus more butter
 for buttering the skillet
1⅓ cups all-purpose flour
½ cup granulated sugar
1 tsp baking powder
1 tsp ground cinnamon
½ tsp ground cloves
½ tsp ground nutmeg
½ tsp fine sea salt
1 large egg
⅔ cup milk
1 tsp pure vanilla extract
10–12 fresh stalks of
 rhubarb, trimmed

Rhubarb is my very favourite of the summer vegetables, and the minute it's in season I start putting it in *everything*. When our family camps, we cook what my boys call "fire food." This cake was born out of a need for some new desserts that could be cooked in a cast iron pan without too much trouble or mess. I've given the method for cooking it in an oven here, but if you're into camping, you can try popping a lid on top and baking this one outdoors (if there's no campfire ban in effect, of course). If you don't love rhubarb as much as I do, any ripe, seasonal fruit will work equally well. —DLA

Preheat the oven to 375°F. Lightly butter a 9-inch cast iron skillet.

In a large mixing bowl, whisk together the flour, sugar, baking powder, cinnamon, cloves, nutmeg, and salt. Make a well in the centre.

In a separate bowl, whisk together the egg, milk, and vanilla. As you whisk, slowly drizzle in the melted butter to combine. Add this milk mixture to the dry ingredients and stir lightly, just to combine.

Pour the batter into the prepared skillet. Cut the rhubarb stalks to fit your pan and lay them on top of the cake batter. Push down very lightly, just enough to embed them but not submerge them.

Bake for 30–35 minutes, or until the cake is golden brown and a skewer inserted into the centre of the cake comes out clean. Remove from the oven and let cool. Serve directly from the pan. This will keep in an airtight container in the fridge for 2–3 days.

Denman Island Chocolate, Beetroot, and Walnut Cake

MAKES 1 TEN-INCH
BUNDT CAKE

Cake

2 medium-sized beets
2 Tbsp plus ⅔ cup unsalted
    butter, melted
2 Tbsp best quality dark
    cocoa
2 cups all-purpose flour
2 tsp baking soda
¼ tsp fine sea salt
1 cup granulated sugar
2 large eggs
1½ cups buttermilk
½ cup strong coffee,
    cooled
1 tsp pure vanilla extract
1 cup roughly chopped
    walnuts (optional)

Glaze

2 cups roughly chopped
    best quality dark
    chocolate
1 cup whipping (35%)
    cream

This may sound like a crazy combination, but trust me, the earthiness of the beets only intensifies the chocolatey goodness and nutty crunch of this glorious cake. The trick is to use really good dark chocolate—my favourite is from Denman Island Chocolate—and to roast the beets to bring out their natural sweetness. —DLA

Preheat the oven to 350°F.

To make the cake, poke the skins of the beets in several places with a fork and then wrap them together in aluminum foil, being sure to seal the package completely. Place the packaged beets in a roasting pan and roast for 45–60 minutes, or until fork-tender. Remove from the oven, unwrap, and let cool completely. Peel and then grate the beets into a bowl, to catch any juices. Set aside.

Rub the inside of a Bundt pan with the 2 Tbsp of butter and then dust with the 2 Tbsp of cocoa to fully coat the inside of the pan. If you're using a truly nonstick pan you might be able to skip this step, but I always do it for good measure.

Preheat the oven to 350°F.

In a large mixing bowl, sieve together the flour, baking soda, and the sea salt. Set aside.

In a stand mixer fitted with the paddle attachment, mix the eggs and the sugar on medium high speed until the sugar is dissolved and the mixture is light yellow. With the mixer running, slowly pour in the ⅔ cup melted butter and then the buttermilk and coffee. Add the beets, and any juices, and the vanilla and mix until just combined.

Add half of the dry ingredients to the wet and mix until just combined. Repeat with the remaining dry ingredients. Do not overmix. Fold in the walnuts (if using).

Pour the batter into the prepared Bundt pan and bake for 50–60 minutes, or until a wooden skewer inserted in the centre of the cake comes out clean. This is a dense, moist cake, so it should be baked through but not overdone.

Place the pan on a cooling rack for at least 15 minutes. Remove the pan from the cooling rack, place the cooling rack on the open side of the inverted pan, and flip over carefully so that the cake is now right side up. Let cool for another 5 minutes and then remove the pan. Let the cake cool completely before frosting.

To make the glaze, place the chocolate and cream in the top of a double boiler, or a large metal mixing bowl set over a gently simmering pan of water, and stir until completely melted. Remove from the heat and let sit for 4–5 minutes, stirring frequently. Pour over the Bundt cake and let settle for 5 minutes before serving.

field

Empress Lavender Gin Fizz

SERVES 2

Lavender simple syrup
½ cup water
½ cup granulated sugar
3 Tbsp fresh lavender
blossoms

Gin fizz
Ice cubes
2 oz gin
3 Tbsp lavender simple
syrup
2 tsp lemon juice
Sparkling water
2 lavender stems to garnish

Is there anything more glorious than the swaths of deep purple from a lavender field in bloom? In this recipe I've tried to bottle that vision up and deliver it to you in a classic cocktail with a twist. The Empress 1908 Gin from Victoria Distillers turns from its glorious bottled indigo colour to a soft pinky-purple, thanks to the citrus, perfectly conveying the soft lavender flavour within. You can, of course, use your favourite gin, but if you can get your hands on the Empress, I highly recommend it. —DLA

To make the simple syrup, place ½ cup water, sugar, and lavender blossoms in a small saucepan over medium heat. Give everything a quick stir to combine and then bring to a simmer. Keep it at a simmer for 10 minutes, being sure not to let it come to a boil. Remove from the heat, let cool completely, and strain the lavender blossoms out. The syrup will keep in an airtight container in the fridge for up to 2 months.

To make the gin fizz, fill a cocktail shaker halfway with ice cubes and pour in the gin, simple syrup, and lemon juice. Shake well. Divide evenly between two champagne cups or martini glasses, top with sparkling water, and stir once to mix. Garnish with a lavender stem and serve immediately.

Spiced Apple Hot Toddy

SERVES 4

3 cups apple juice

1-inch piece ginger

1 large apple, peeled,
   cored, and chopped

¼ cup pure maple syrup

2 tsp fennel seeds

6 whole cloves

4 cardamom pods

4 cinnamon sticks

2 star anise

Coarse sea salt

1 lemon

4 oz spiced rum or brandy

Here's something to warm you from the inside out on a dark, wet winter night. Local fresh ginger is hotter than store-bought and spices up this drink to make it the perfect cold remedy. Vancouver Island is home to many heritage apple varieties that offer unique sweet and tart flavours. Pink Lady and Salish store well, and are available during the winter. Experiment until you find your favourite varietal. This recipe doubles or triples easily, and if you're having a party, try keeping it in a slow cooker (after you've strained it). It will stay warm all evening and your guests can top up their glasses as they wish. —EL

In a large saucepan over low heat, warm the apple juice, but don't let it boil. Peel and slice the ginger. Add the ginger, apple, maple syrup, fennel seeds, cloves, cardamom pods, cinnamon sticks, star anise, and a pinch of salt to the warmed juice.

Slice the lemon into rounds. Add half to the pan, increase the heat to medium, and bring to a slow boil. Cover, turn down the heat to low, and simmer for 20–30 minutes, until the apple is soft, and the spices are plump. Of course, it will smell heavenly.

Remove from the heat and pour the mixture through a fine mesh strainer into a large bowl. Remove the larger spices from the strainer (keeping the cinnamon sticks intact—give them a quick rinse and set aside). Then, using a spoon, press the apple flesh through the strainer. Whisk to emulsify and incorporate the cooked apple. Return the spiced apple juice mixture to the pan and keep warm until ready to serve.

Make a cut from the centre to the peels of the remaining lemon rounds. Divide the rum (or brandy) between four mugs and top with warm spiced apple juice. Garnish each mug with a lemon round on its rim and a cinnamon stick.

This will keep in an airtight container in the fridge for up to 1 week.

field

field

fai

farm

Since the introduction of domesticated livestock to the Island in the mid-nineteenth century, animal husbandry has been a mainstay of commercial farming and food here. In fact, the Island was home to BC's first dairy cooperative, the Cowichan Creamery, which opened its doors in 1895. One hundred and twenty-four years later, the dairy industry is still going strong. Nowadays, we're spoiled for choices in cheese as Vancouver Island cheesemakers offer a number of award-winning varieties from local producers such as Natural Pastures Cheese Company and Little Qualicum Cheeseworks; small-scale producers with wide-reaching distribution, such as Salt Spring Island Cheese Company and Haltwhistle Cheese Company in Duncan, are becoming renowned for their traditional methods and innovative flavours. Yogurt made here is also making waves on the Island and across the country, with artisans like Tree Island and the delicious buffalo milk product crafted by McClintock's Farm in the Comox Valley, proving that our grass-fed cattle produces insanely delicious milk.

The movement towards pasture-raised and heritage-bred meats has deep roots here, and our farmers work hard to ensure the preservation of animal lineage. The folks at End of the Road Ranch raise Large Blacks, an endangered heirloom breed of pig that provides the meat most similar to wild boar anywhere—in fact, the grandsire to the farm's top breeding male was a boar from the Saurita Lake group of wild pigs. Jessie and Evelyn of Terra Nossa Organic Farms raise chickens that spend their time in vast green pastures, and piglets that smile at visitors through a sea of wildflowers. Lamb from Salt Spring Island is now famous far beyond its humble shores. In addition to the traditional meats of pork, chicken, beef, and turkey, Vancouver Island is also home to both water buffalo in the Comox Valley and the Morning Star Bison Ranch just outside of Nanaimo, offering consumers one of the widest ranges of meat cuts available on a local scale throughout North America.

Of course, not every farmer here produces meat or dairy. The humble honeybee has a big role to play throughout the Gulf Islands, not just for its pollination skills—necessary for the vast array of crops grown here—but also for the outstanding golden honeys that bees produce. Farmers are now supplying honey which is being incorporated into everything from spirits made in local distilleries to honey-flavored yogurt varieties; meaderies that craft honey-based wines have grown throughout the Islands, many with tasting rooms dedicated to bee education.

But this has long been the practice here: small-scale farmers working with love and passion to humanely raise animals, educate consumers, and create exceptional products. This is our way of life, and it comes through in the quality and flavours that make our islands' farms so distinct. Along the winding country roads of Sooke, Metchosin, the Cowichan and Comox valleys, and in almost every small village across the Gulf Islands, roadside stands laden with milk, produce, and fresh eggs for sale are readily available. Backyard chickens, small sharehold farmers, and larger-scale free-range organic producers, such as James and Cammy of Lockwood Farms, work together to bring the best of Island foods to Island families. We hope you'll enjoy these recipes that celebrate our meat, dairy, egg, and honey farmers; may you feel a deep sense of the love and care with which they raise their stocks and craft their exceptional products. —DLA

farm

Farm Eggs Island-Style

with Cherry Tomatoes and Roasted Asparagus

SERVES 4

8 stalks asparagus, woody
   ends trimmed
Handful of cherry
   tomatoes
4–5 Tbsp extra virgin olive
   oil, divided
Flaked sea salt
½ medium cooking onion,
   diced
1 clove garlic, minced
1 tsp chili powder
3 cups canned black beans,
   drained and rinsed
½ cup water, plus more
   if needed
1 cup sour cream
1 canned chipotle
   pepper, finely chopped
   (optional)
8 corn tortillas
8 large farm-fresh eggs
2 cups grated Monterey
   Jill cheese
1 large bunch of cilantro,
   coarsely chopped
Salsa for serving

This is our Island version of huevos rancheros which translates literally to ranch eggs. It is my husband's preferred way to use the gloriously fresh eggs we're lucky enough to get from our chickens. I love to add whatever is fresh from the fields, but this is my favourite variation. If you don't like your food very spicy, you can leave out the chipotle and just add plain sour cream at the end. I also call for Monterey Jill cheese from Little Qualicum Cheeseworks here, but you can use any cheese you like. —DLA

Preheat the oven to 400°F.

On a rimmed cookie sheet, toss the asparagus and cherry tomatoes with 1 Tbsp of the olive oil and a sprinkle of salt. Roast for 10 minutes, turn over, and roast for another 5 minutes. Remove from the heat and wrap loosely in aluminum foil to keep warm.

Place a large skillet over medium-high heat and add 2 Tbsp oil. Once the oil is warm, add the onion and garlic and sauté until the onion begins to soften, 1–2 minutes. Mix in the chili powder and cook for another minute. Add the beans and water. Mix to combine and then turn down the heat to medium. Simmer, without boiling, for 5 minutes or so, until the liquid begins to be absorbed, and then begin mashing the beans with the back of a spoon. If the mixture gets too dry, add a bit more water, 1 Tbsp at a time. The beans are done after 20–25 minutes. They should be a garlicky, chunky mash. Remove from the pan and cover to keep warm.

In a small bowl, mix the sour cream with the chipotle pepper (if using). Set aside, uncovered, at room temperature.

Add enough oil to a clean skillet over medium-high heat to just coat the bottom of the pan. Fry the tortillas, one at a time, until they start to puff up, 5–10 seconds per tortilla. Flip, repeat, and then set on a paper towel to drain. Repeat with all the tortillas.

In the same skillet (no need to wipe it out first), use the remaining oil to fry the eggs over medium-high heat to slightly runny sunny-side up (any style of eggs will do here. If if you prefer scrambled, then go ahead and scramble them).

To assemble, top each tortilla with the warm refried black beans, cheese, and two eggs. Top with the roasted asparagus, cherry tomatoes, a small handful of cilantro, a spoonful of salsa, and a drizzle of chipotle sour cream. Serve immediately.

You can store the chipotle sour cream in an airtight container in the fridge for up to 7 days.

farm

Smoked Bacon, Asparagus, and Roasted Shallot Quiche

MAKES ONE ROUND
8-INCH QUICHE OR
ONE 12- X 14-INCH
RECTANGULAR TART

Pastry

1½ cups all-purpose flour

1 tsp coarse sea salt

1 tsp chopped rosemary
 leaves

½ cup salted butter, chilled
 and cubed

1 egg

1 tsp white vinegar

2 Tbsp cold water

Filling

6 large shallots

2 Tbsp extra virgin olive oil

½ tsp fine sea salt

4 strips smoked bacon

6 eggs

½ cup Greek yogurt

1 tsp cracked black pepper

½ cup grated Qualicum
 Spice cheese

8–10 stalks asparagus, ends
 trimmed

Perfect for weekend brunch or a simple weeknight dinner, quiche is filling yet light. I love to make this version in a long tart pan, cutting slices rather than wedges, to show off the beautiful asparagus, but it looks beautiful in an 8-inch pie plate as well. (Note: If Qualicum spiced cheese isn't available, your favourite herbed cheese or Monterey Jack would be good substitutes.)—EL

To make the pastry, place the flour in a large bowl. In a mortar, grind the salt and rosemary with a pestle to form a coarse mixture. Whisk this into the flour and then add the butter. Using a pastry blender or two knives, cut the butter into the flour mixture until it resembles coarse oatmeal.

In a measuring cup, and using a fork, whisk the egg with the vinegar. Gently whisk in cold water and pour it all over the flour mixture. Carefully mix the wet and dry ingredients together by folding and pressing the pastry into the bowl. Be careful not to overmix. When the pastry just comes together into a ball, wrap it in plastic wrap and refrigerate for 30 minutes, or up to overnight.

Preheat the oven to 350°F. Place one rack in the bottom third of the oven and another in the centre.

Remove the dough from the fridge and turn it out onto a lightly floured surface. Roll it into a 10-inch circle (or 14- × 6-inch rectangle). Carefully roll up the pastry over the rolling pin and place it in a pie dish. Press it into the pan, crimping it around the edges. Line the shell with foil and cover with pie weights or a heavy dish. Bake for 8 minutes, or until golden. Remove from the oven and allow to cool slightly before removing the foil.

Line a rimmed baking sheet with parchment paper.

Peel the shallots and slice them lengthwise to expose the layers. Place the shallots on the baking sheet, drizzle with oil, and sprinkle with salt. Roast on the bottom rack of the oven for about 45 minutes.

While the shallots are roasting, slice the bacon into ½-inch pieces and fry over medium heat until just crisp. Drain on paper towel and set aside.

In a large mixing bowl or liquid measuring cup, whisk together the eggs, yogurt, and pepper until completely smooth and lump-free. Stir in the cheese. Pour this egg mixture into the pie crust and scatter the crisped bacon evenly overtop. Arrange the asparagus overtop of the bacon bits.

Bake in the centre of the oven for 20 minutes if using a rectangular tart pan, or 30–35 minutes if using a round pie dish. The quiche is ready when a knife inserted in the centre comes out clean.

Remove the quiche and the shallots from the oven. Let rest for 3 minutes, then arrange the shallots on the top of the quiche and serve immediately.

Coffee-Glazed Apple Bacon Fritters

MAKES 12 FRITTERS

1 Tbsp salted butter

3 tart apples, peeled, cored, and cut into ½-inch chunks

12 slices thick-cut bacon, cooked and cooled

1¼ cups all-purpose flour

1½ tsp baking powder

½ tsp fine sea salt

½ tsp ground anise

1 large egg

¼ cup granulated sugar

½ cup sparkling apple juice

2 cups icing sugar

¼ cup extra-strong coffee or espresso, cooled

Vegetable oil, for frying

My husband, James, loves apple fritters. And bacon. And coffee. So it wasn't a stretch to think that combining the three into one delicious treat would be a great idea. Salty, sweet, and just a hint of smokiness are my go-to flavours when I really want to indulge and use up the glut of apples that appear in our orchard every autumn. As with any recipe, the taste will depend on the quality of the ingredients you use, so I highly recommend seeking out a good quality, thick-cut bacon—our family loves Hertel Meats—and firm, tart, local apples. —DLA

In a saucepan over medium heat, melt the butter and let it cook until it is light golden. Add the apples and cook, turning frequently, until they just begin to soften and deepen in colour, 7–8 minutes. Do not let them cook all the way through—you want them soft but with a bit of crunch. Remove from the heat and transfer to a mixing bowl. Crumble the bacon into the apples, stir to combine, and set aside.

In a large mixing bowl, sieve the flour with the baking powder, salt, and ground anise. Set aside.

In a separate large mixing bowl, whisk the egg with the sugar until they turn a light golden colour. Add the apples and bacon to the wet ingredients and mix to combine.

Pour the wet ingredients into the dry and, using a spatula or wooden spoon, stir slightly until just combined. Add the sparkling apple juice and give it all a final stir to combine.

In another mixing bowl, whisk the icing sugar with the coffee to make a glaze. Set aside.

Place a wire rack over a rimmed baking sheet. Line another baking sheet with paper towel.

Add 3–4 inches of vegetable oil to a Dutch oven over medium heat. Warm the oil to 350°F. Working quickly, use two tablespoons to scoop up some batter and carefully drop it into the oil. Cook three to four fritters at a time. Cook for about 2 minutes, or until deeply golden on one side. Flip over and cook the other side for another minute or two, until each side is evenly coloured. Remove from the oil and let drain on the paper towel.

While the fritters are still warm, dip them into the coffee glaze, let the excess drain off, and place on the wire rack to set.

These will keep in an airtight container in the fridge for up to 5 days. To get them crispy again, preheat the oven to 350°F, place the fritters on a parchment-lined baking tray, and place in the oven for 10–12 minutes.

Stuffed Red Fife Crêpes
with Prosciutto, Pear, and Buffalo Mozzarella

SERVES 4

2 eggs

1 cup whole milk

¼ cup salted butter, melted, plus more for the pan

¾ cup Red Fife flour

½ tsp fine sea salt

2 Bartlett pears

2 large fresh mozzarella balls

8 slices prosciutto

8 sprigs of thyme, leaves only

2 tsp minced chives

Cracked black pepper

Savoury crepes are so versatile! I just love them. Hearty and rich, these make a decadent brunch or a light main course, depending on your mood. My mood is always happy when I know these are about to land on the table. The Red Fife flour (see page 33) adds a natural nuttiness to the crêpes and ensures that every bite you take will offer the perfect, delicious balance between salty prosciutto, sweet crunchy pear, and soft creamy buffalo milk cheese. I buy my buffalo milk cheese from McClintock's Farm in Courtney.

If you can't get Red Fife flour, use your favourite whole wheat flour instead. —EL

Place the eggs, milk, and butter in a blender and add the flour and salt. Pulse just until combined and then blend on high speed for 30 seconds. Pour into a mixing bowl, cover with plastic wrap, making sure it touches the surface of the batter, and refrigerate for 30–60 minutes.

Cut eight sheets of parchment paper or wax paper, 6 × 6 inches, and set aside. These will be used to stack the crêpes so they don't stick.

Heat a medium-sized nonstick skillet over medium-high heat, add 1 tsp of butter, swirl to coat the pan evenly, and turn down the heat to medium. Remove the batter from the fridge.

Pour in ¼ cup of batter and swirl the pan quickly so the batter coats it in one even layer. When the batter looks set and small bubbles are starting to form on top, use an offset spatula to carefully lift the edge of the crêpe. To do this, hold the edge gently with your fingers—it will be warm but not too hot—and lift it slightly, slipping the spatula underneath. Flip the crêpe over, cook for an additional 30–45 seconds, then carefully lift the edge, slipping the spatula under the crêpe again, and transfer gently to sit on a parchment square. Place another piece of parchment on top. Repeat with the remaining batter, stacking the crêpes on top of each other with parchment sheets in between. You should have eight crêpes.

Peel, quarter, and core the pears then slice each quarter in half lengthwise. Slice each mozzarella ball into four rounds, then slice each round in half, creating 16 half-moons.

Preheat the oven to 350°F. Turn it off as soon as it reaches temperature.

Take the top crêpe from the stack and place a slice of prosciutto along the centre. Top with two slices of pear, then two half-moons of mozzarella. Sprinkle with the leaves from one sprig of thyme, a pinch of chives, and a pinch of pepper. The filling should be neatly stacked in a line along the centre. There should be some prosciutto showing at either end.

Fold the bottom and top of the crêpe over the filling and then fold over each of the sides, as if you were folding a burrito. Carefully flip the crêpe and place it fold side down on a serving plate. Repeat with the remaining

crêpes. As you work, place two crêpes on a serving plate and put each plate in the oven to keep them warm and gently melt the cheese.

Once the last plate has gone into the oven, let rest in the oven for 5 minutes before serving.

These will keep in the fridge overnight, but they're best eaten as soon as they come out of the oven.

Spruce-Rubbed Bison Carpaccio
with Wild Plum Reduction

1 Tbsp chopped fresh
   spruce needles

1 tsp mustard seeds

1 tsp caraway seeds

1 Tbsp coarse sea salt

2 tsp black peppercorns

1 lb bison loin

2 Tbsp extra virgin olive oil

2 cups pitted and chopped
   wild plums

¼ cup water

½ cup red wine

¼ cup granulated sugar

Flaked sea salt and cracked
   black pepper

Dry aged cheese, such
   as Natural Pastures'
   Boerenkaas for garnish

Bison is an incredibly tender and absolutely delicious meat, and we're lucky enough to have Morning Star Bison Ranch right here outside of Nanaimo as a local source. If you like the complexity of a good bison burger, you'll love this. And if you've never tried bison, one taste of this and you'll see why it has become a staple in our home. Any sharp, dry Tomme cheese will do, but I like to use Natural Pastures Cheese Company's Boerenkaas for the cheese. —DLA

Place the spruce needles, mustard seeds, and caraway seeds in a mortar with the salt and pepper. Grind with the pestle until you have a coarse powder.

Rub the bison loin all over with the oil and then rub the spruce mixture in firmly to coat it. Set aside.

Heat a cast iron pan or a large skillet over medium-high heat and sear the loin on all sides until a good crust is formed, about 1 minute per side. Remove the loin from the pan and let cool at room temperature. Once it's cool to the touch, wrap it tightly in plastic wrap to create a cylindrical shape. Wrap again in aluminum foil and place in the freezer overnight.

Place the plums and water in a non-reactive saucepan set over medium heat. Cook until the plums begin to break down and become syrupy, about 10 minutes. Remove from the heat and press the plums through a sieve or food mill. Discard the solids left in the sieve. Place the sieved juices, the wine, and sugar back into the pan, set over medium heat, and simmer until a syrupy consistency is formed, 15–20 minutes. Remove from the heat and set aside to cool completely.

To serve, remove the bison loin from the freezer and unwrap. Using a meat slicer or very sharp knife, slice the loin into paper-thin rounds. Arrange the carpaccio on a plate, drizzle with the wild plum reduction, and garnish with a pinch of salt, a pinch of pepper, and a handful of cheese shavings. Enjoy right away!

farm

Apple Brandy-Spiked Chicken Liver Pâté

SERVES 4

4 Tbsp salted butter, divided

1 small red onion, diced

1 large tart apple, peeled, cored, and roughly chopped

½ tsp coarse sea salt

2 Tbsp lemon juice

1 lb chicken livers

2 sprigs thyme

½ tsp pink peppercorns

½ cup whipping (35%) cream

½ tsp ground black pepper

¼ tsp ground nutmeg

¼ cup apple brandy or calvados

We're lucky to have an abundance of grain–fed, free-range chickens on Vancouver Island. Their livers have a mild flavour, which is softened further in this recipe by the cream. The apple adds sweetness and the brandy a delightful layer of complexity. If you can, try to use apple brandy from Merridale Cidery & Distillery in the Cowichan Valley. It's incredible here. This is simple enough for every day and perfect for special occasions. —EL

In a saucepan over medium heat, melt 2 Tbsp of the butter. Add the onion, stirring frequently, for 2–3 minutes. Add the apple, sprinkle with salt, and sauté until the apple is golden on the outside but still holding its shape, about 5 minutes. Sprinkle the lemon juice overtop and deglaze the pan, scraping up any bits that have stuck to the bottom. Transfer this mixture to a blender.

Wash and dry the chicken livers. Carefully remove any veins, pieces of sinew, or dark spots.

Place the remaining 2 Tbsp of butter in the pan and set it over medium-high heat. When it is melted, add the livers. Sauté for 5 minutes, stirring well to ensure they don't stick, until they're firm on the outside and pink on the inside. Remove from the heat but leave them in the pan.

Remove the leaves from the sprigs of thyme. Place them in a mortar with the pink peppercorns and crush with a pestle.

Pour the cream over the chicken livers and stir in the crushed thyme and peppercorns, pepper, and nutmeg. Place the pan over medium-high heat, bring to almost a boil, pour in the brandy, and simmer until the pan juices reduce, about 3 minutes. The livers are done when no pink remains.

Add the livers and all the pan juices to the blender with the apple and onion mixture. Purée until completely smooth and pour into a 2–3 cup serving dish. Cover with plastic wrap, making it sure it touches the surface of the pâté. Chill for at least 6 hours.

This will keep in an airtight container in the fridge for up to 3 days.

Hazelnut-Crusted Chèvre
with Blackberry Sage Compote

MAKES 8 DISCS
(SERVES 4)

Compote

2 cups blackberries, fresh
  or frozen
½ cup granulated sugar
¼ cup finely chopped sage
  leaves

Chèvre

2 cups chèvre
2 cups all-purpose flour
3 eggs, lightly beaten
2 cups finely chopped
  hazelnuts
Vegetable oil spray

This recipe is a bit of a process, but it's well worth the effort. Just wait until you taste the fresh goat cheese encrusted with freshly harvested local hazelnuts. This makes a perfect light lunch served with a green salad or is a good starter for a more formal dinner —DLA

To make the compote, in a heavy-bottomed saucepan over medium heat, cook the blackberries and sugar with the sage until the sugar has dissolved and the fruit is just starting to break down—approximately 15 minutes. The compote should be syrupy and still chunky.

To prepare the chèvre, separate it into eight evenly sized portions. Using your hands, form each one into a 1-inch-thick disc. Cover with plastic wrap and refrigerate for at least 1 hour, or up to overnight.

Preheat the oven to 400°F. Line a baking sheet with parchment paper.

Set up a dredging station: place the flour, eggs, and hazelnuts in separate shallow bowls. Take the chèvre from the fridge and, working with one piece at a time, dip each disc in the flour, coating fully and shaking off any excess; dip in the egg, coating fully and shaking off the excess; and finally, set them on top of the hazelnuts, pressing down slightly to coat. Turn them over to coat the other side as well.

Place the hazelnut-crusted chèvre discs on the prepared baking sheet and spray them lightly with vegetable oil. Flip them over and spray the other side.

Bake for 5 minutes, turn over, and bake for another 5 minutes. Serve hot or cold with the compote on the side.

You can store the compote in an airtight container in the fridge for up to 1 week. The cooked chèvre discs can be stored in an airtight container in the fridge for up to a week. Reheat them at 375°F for 10–12 minutes before eating.

farm

Homemade Ricotta

with Red Currant Compote, Honeycomb, and Lemon Thyme

MAKES 1½ CUPS

Ricotta Cheese
2 cups whole milk
2 cups whipping (35%)
    cream
¼ cup lemon juice (1–2
    lemons)
1 tsp sea salt

Red Currant Compote
1½ cups fresh or frozen
    red currants, stems
    discarded
¼ cup honey
2 Tbsp lemon juice
½ tsp fine sea salt
¼ cup crumbled
    honeycomb
4 sprigs lemon thyme,
    leaves only

It's actually quite simple to make ricotta cheese at home, and it's especially good if you use locally sourced milk or cream. Remember, the longer you leave it to drain, the thicker the ricotta will be. If you want the texture to be a little more like mascarpone, substitute one cup of milk for the cream. As for the compote, you could also use sweet or sour cherries instead of red currants. Just cut the honey in half if you're using sweet cherries. —EL

In a large, heavy-bottomed saucepan over medium heat, warm the milk and cream. Stirring constantly, heat the liquid until a candy thermometer shows 190°F.

Remove from the heat and add the lemon juice and salt. Give one gentle stir to incorporate everything and then let the mixture stand for 10 minutes without stirring or moving it at all.

Line a fine mesh strainer with a few layers of cheesecloth, allowing the edges to hang over the sides, and place it over a large bowl. Gently pour the milk mixture (which will now be curds and whey—don't be alarmed by its appearance!) into the cheesecloth and allow to stand, uncovered, for at least 2 hours, to allow the curds to fully set and the whey to drain off. Pull up the sides of the cheesecloth to gently squeeze any extra whey into the bowl, leaving only ricotta in the cheesecloth.

Discard the whey and transfer the ricotta to an airtight container. You can store it in the fridge for up to 1 week.

Place the red currants in a small saucepan set over medium heat. Drizzle with the honey, lemon juice, and salt. Bring to a simmer and then cook, uncovered, for 5 minutes. Crush the currants gently with a spatula to break them up. Increase heat to medium-high, bring to a boil, and let boil for 2 minutes, until the currants soften and the juices have reduced a little. Remove from the heat and let cool completely.

Spoon the ricotta into a serving bowl, spoon the red currant compote overtop, and garnish with honeycomb and thyme leaves.

Serve immediately with crackers or toasts.

All the components will keep in separate airtight containers in the fridge for up to 1 week. Once you have combined them, they are best enjoyed the day they are made.

farm

Ferryman's Lunch Platter

This isn't really a recipe, more of a great lunch suggestion in my opinion. It's a spin on the classic ploughman's lunch that I've named the Ferryman's Lunch in honour of our hardworking BC Ferries folk who keep Vancouver Island and our local Gulf Islands coming and going.

I like to keep things as local as I can by using charcuterie and cheeses from the many producers here on the Islands, and places like SaltSpring Kitchen Co. are my go-to for pickles, jams, and jellies.

The possible combinations for this are limitless, but look for a balance between opposites, for both tastes and textures for best results. Aim for a good mix of soft and crunchy, salty and sweet, moist and dry. As for quantities, you know your own appetite, so use that as your guide when you're arranging your plate. Here I've given you lists of possible components. It's up to you how much of each one you want to use. —DLA

Meats
Dry cured meat, such as salami, dry chorizo, or dry beef carpaccio
Soft cured meat, such as honey ham, smoked turkey breast, mortadella
Soft meat, such as pâté, rillettes, liverwurst

Cheeses
Soft cheese, such as Brie, Camembert, or Gorgonzola
Hard cheese, such as Tomme, cheddar, or Monterey Jack
Fresh cheese, such as chèvre or feta
Blue cheese, such as Stilton, Bleu Claire, or Blue Juliette

Pickles and accompaniments
Our Quick Summer Farm Pickles are perfect (page 44)
Jelly, jam, or mustard

To serve
An assortment of breads and crackers

Valley Farmer Pot Pies

SERVES 6

Pastry

2 cups all-purpose flour

½ tsp fine sea salt

1 cup unsalted cold butter,
  cubed

¼ cup ice water, plus more
  if needed

1 Tbsp white vinegar

Milk, for brushing

Chicken filling

6 Tbsp unsalted butter,
  softened, divided

1 small cooking onion,
  finely chopped

1 carrot, peeled and diced

1 stalk celery, diced

¼ cup all-purpose flour

2 cups chicken stock

½ lb Yukon gold potatoes,
  peeled and diced

1 bay leaf

1½ cups diced cooked
  chicken

1 cup frozen peas

1 cup pearl onions,
  blanched and peeled

Fine sea salt and cracked
  black pepper

The first food I can remember eating is my mom's chicken pot pie; it was warm and comforting and would come to define homey comfort food for me as I became an adult. My dad, who's English, instilled a love for a steak pie in me, and my husband is obsessed with all things pig, so we have a lot of pork going through the kitchen. Luckily, with all of the beautiful pasture-raised meats that are reared here on Vancouver Island, I'm spoiled for choice when it comes to using all these meats as pie fillings. I couldn't decide which variation to give you, so I've included options for using beef or pork as well as chicken. I'll leave it to you to decide which is your favourite. —DLA

To make the pastry, place the flour and salt in a food processor. Pulse twice just to combine. Add the butter in one addition and pulse for a few seconds at a time until the butter is the size of peas. Add ice water and vinegar, and pulse again until the dough just begins to form. Add more ice-cold water, 1 Tbsp at a time, if needed. Turn the dough out onto a lightly floured work surface. Using your hands, form the pastry into two discs. Wrap the discs tightly in plastic wrap and refrigerate for 30 minutes.

To make the filling, in a large saucepan over medium heat, melt 3 Tbsp of the butter and then add the chopped onions, carrots, and celery. Cook, stirring, just until the vegetables begin to soften, 8–10 minutes. Remove the vegetables from the pan and set aside. In the same pan, melt the remaining 3 Tbsp of butter over medium heat and then add the flour. Cook, stirring constantly with a wooden spoon, for 5–6 minutes, or until the flour begins to brown and has a slightly nutty aroma. Slowly pour in the broth, whisking constantly to combine.

Bring the broth to a boil over medium heat and add the potatoes and bay leaf. Return to a low boil, cover, and simmer, uncovered, for about 15 minutes, or until the potatoes are fork-tender. Stir in the chicken, peas, onions, and salt and pepper to taste.

Preheat oven to 375°F. On a well-floured work surface, roll out the two discs of dough into 12-inch circles and line a 9-inch pie plate with one of them. Pour the pie filling into the crust. Brush around the edges of the dough with milk and cover with the second sheet of pastry. Crimp the edges and brush with milk. Cut three or four 1-inch slits in the top of the pastry to allow the steam to escape.

Bake for about 50 minutes, or until the pastry is golden brown. Let rest for 15 minutes before serving.

Leftovers can be stored, tightly covered, in the fridge for 3–4 days.

Variations

Beef: Replace the chicken stock with 1 cup beef stock plus 1 cup dark porter beer, and replace the chicken with 1½ cups diced cooked steak or ground beef.

Pork: Use 1 cup chicken stock plus 1 cup apple juice, add ½ cup chopped dried apricots, and replace the chicken with 1½ cups diced cooked pork loin.

Aged Cheddar, Smoked Ham, and Apple Galette

SERVES 6–8

Pastry

1½ cups all-purpose flour

2 Tbsp thyme leaves

½ tsp fine sea salt

½ cup cold unsalted butter,
cut into 1-inch cubes

5–6 Tbsp cold water

1 large egg

1 Tbsp milk

Filling

1 Tbsp salted butter

2 Tbsp all-purpose flour

¾ cups milk

2 Tbsp grainy mustard

2 cups grated aged cheddar
cheese

1 cup (1-inch) cubed
smoked ham

2–3 large baking apples,
cored, cut into ¼-inch
slices (peel left on)

1 tsp grated lemon zest

Flaked sea salt and cracked
black pepper

This galette is a delicious combination of sharp aged cheddar, salty ham, and sweet apples. You can sub in any of your favourite cheeses, but I prefer the smooth depth of a good, aged cheddar. Paradise Island Cheeses are a big favourite of mine. Serve this with a green salad for a delicious lunch or topped with a fried egg for a special breakfast treat. —DLA

To make the pastry, place the flour, thyme, and salt in a food processor. Pulse once to combine. Add all the butter and pulse a few more times until the mixture is crumbly and the butter is cut down into pea-sized pieces. Add the cold water, 1 Tbsp at a time, pulsing in between to bring the dough together.

Dump the dough out onto a piece of plastic wrap and form it into a disc. Wrap it tightly and refrigerate for at least 30 minutes.

Preheat the oven to 425°F. Line a rimmed baking sheet with parchment paper.

To make the filling, first melt the butter in a saucepan over medium heat and add the flour. Stir to combine and cook until the flour begins to brown and has a slightly nutty aroma. While whisking constantly, add the milk and continue to stir until the roux thickens. Remove from the heat and add the grainy mustard. Set aside.

In a large bowl, place the cheese, ham, apple slices, lemon zest, and a pinch of salt and pepper. Toss lightly just to combine.

Place the dough on a well-floured work surface and roll it into a 12-inch circle. Transfer the dough to the prepared baking sheet.

Spread the mustard roux over the middle of the pastry, leaving a 2-inch-wide border along the perimeter. Top with the cheese, ham, and apple mixture. Fold the bare edges of the dough in towards the centre to form a rustic crust.

Make an egg wash by beating the egg with the milk. Brush the crust with the egg wash and bake the galette for 25–30 minutes, or until the crust is golden brown and the filling is bubbling.

Remove the galette from the oven and allow to cool in the pan for 5–10 minutes before serving.

Leftovers will keep in an airtight container in the fridge for up to 1 week.

Tea-Brined Chicken, Blueberry, and Corn Salad

SERVES 6–8

Chicken

4 cups water
6 Tbsp loose black tea or 6 tea bags
½ cup packed Demerara sugar
¼ cup fine sea salt
4 boneless, skinless chicken breasts
2 Tbsp olive oil

Dressing

½ cup lime juice (from about 4 limes)
2 Tbsp honey
Fine sea salt and cracked black pepper

Salad

Kernels cut from 6 ears of fresh corn
8 cups blueberries
1 small red onion, diced
Large handful roughly chopped cilantro

This is a variation of my friend Lesley Stowe's legendary salad. I make this every summer when the first peaches and cream corn begins to arrive from our local farms. Any black tea variety will work well here, but a bergamot mixture from the Westholme Tea Farm is my favourite. —DLA

To prepare the chicken, in a large saucepan, boil the water. Add the tea, sugar, and salt. Stir and set aside to cool, about 30 minutes. Strain the liquid through a fine mesh sieve into a large resealable plastic bag. Add the chicken, seal tightly, and refrigerate overnight. The next day, remove the chicken and discard the marinade.

Preheat the oven to 400°F.

In a cast iron or other oven-safe skillet over medium-high heat, warm the oil and sear the chicken breasts, smooth side down, until a golden crust appears, 4–5 minutes. Repeat on the other side. Place the skillet in the oven for 10–12 minutes, or until the chicken is cooked through. Transfer the chicken to a plate to rest for at least 15 minutes.

To make the dressing, combine the lime juice, honey, salt, and pepper in a bowl.

To make the salad, in a large bowl, mix together the corn, blueberries, onion, and cilantro. Slice the chicken breasts and add to the vegetables along with the dressing. Toss and let sit for at least 5 minutes to meld the flavours.

This will keep in an airtight container in the fridge for up to 4 days.

Cedar-Grilled Spatchcock Herb-Rubbed Chicken

SERVES 4

1 (7–10 lb) roasting
   chicken
1 Tbsp plus 1 tsp coarse
   sea salt
1 cup salted butter
2 Tbsp lemon juice
1 Tbsp honey
2 Tbsp chopped oregano
   leaves
2 Tbsp chopped rosemary
   leaves
1 Tbsp thyme leaves
¼ cup chopped fresh
   parsley (flat-leaf or
   curly)
1 lb cedar wood chips

The simplest way to cook a whole chicken on a grill is to take out the spine and roast it flat. The chicken will cook evenly and quickly. If cedar chips aren't easily accessible, any wood chips will do to add a smoky rustic flavour. (Note: You can also cook this in the oven. Preheat the oven to 425°F and place the chicken in a roasting pan. Roast, uncovered, on the bottom rack of the oven for 35–40 minutes, or until the internal temperature is 145°F.) —EL

Rinse the chicken in hot water and pat it thoroughly dry with paper towels. Using very sharp shears, cut out the spine of the chicken and separate the legs to lay it flat on a cutting board, skin side down. Dry the inside thoroughly and sprinkle the open cavity with the 1 Tbsp of salt. Rub the salt into the cavity and let rest.

In a mixing bowl, beat the butter until light and fluffy. Add the lemon juice and honey, beating to combine. Place the oregano, rosemary, and thyme in a mortar with the remaining 1 tsp salt. Grind them to create a fine green salt. Add this to the butter mixture, then add the parsley and mix well.

Turn the chicken over and pat the skin dry again. Lift the skin from the edge of the breast, making an opening between the skin and the meat. Using your hands, smear some butter under the skin. Ensure your hands and the meat are dry. Repeat with the other breast and each leg. Take 1 Tbsp of the butter and rub it all over the skin.

Heat a grill to 450°F. Place the wood chips in a barbecue basket over the hottest part of the grill and spritz with water to smoke. Cover the barbecue to allow smoke to build, about 5 minutes.

Place the chicken cavity side down on the grill and cover quickly with the lid. Roast for 20 minutes, until well charred. Keeping the lid closed, turn down the grill element directly under the chicken to medium-low. Roast the chicken for another 20–25 minutes. Open the lid of the grill and use a pastry brush to smear any remaining compound butter onto the skin. Roast for 5 more minutes, allowing the skin to crisp up fully. The thickest part of the chicken will register 145°F on a meat thermometer when it's ready.

Remove from the heat and cut the chicken into four to six pieces. Serve immediately.

Leftovers will keep in an airtight container for up to 3 days.

Honey-Roasted Rosemary Garlic Chicken Legs

MAKES 6

½ cup lemon juice (from about 4 lemons)
¼ cup liquid honey
3 Tbsp extra virgin olive oil
4–5 garlic cloves, minced
¼ cup finely chopped rosemary leaves
6 skin-on chicken legs, thighs attached
Flake sea salt to finish

I'm not sure why this recipe is so wildly popular in our house. Maybe it's the sweet tang of our locally harvested, clover-laced honey, or the deep savoury notes of the rosemary and garlic from our garden. Personally, I think it's the magical combination of sweet and savoury flavours bringing out all that's best in a truly free-range chicken. You can marinate this dish up to a day before you plan to eat it. The longer the meat sits, the more time the acid from the lemons has to tenderize it. —DLA

Place the lemon juice, honey, and oil in an extra-large resealable plastic bag (or a large casserole dish). Add the garlic and rosemary and mix well to combine. Add the chicken legs and coat well with the lemon-honey mixture. Marinate in the fridge for at least 4 hours, and up to 24 hours.

Preheat the oven to 375°F. Line a large rimmed baking sheet with parchment paper.

Remove the chicken from the marinade, shake off any excess, and place the legs in a single layer on the baking sheet. Pour a little of the marinade over the legs and discard the remainder.

Bake the chicken for 15 minutes. Brush the tops of the chicken with the juices and marinade that is lying at the bottom of the baking sheet with a pastry or sauce brush. Do this every 15 minutes for 45–50 minutes baking time in total. The chicken is done when the skin is crispy and deeply golden brown. Sprinkle lightly with the salt and serve.

This will keep in an airtight container in the fridge for up to 4 days.

farm

Roasted Duck Breast
with Sticky Sesame Sauce and Braised Broccolini

SERVES 4

Sauce

¼ cup lime juice
(from 2–3 limes)
¼ cup soy sauce
¼ cup honey
3 Tbsp cider vinegar
2 Tbsp cornstarch
2 Tbsp tomato paste
2 large cloves garlic,
minced
1½ tsp ground ginger
3 Tbsp toasted sesame oil
4 ripe plums
1 tsp black sesame seeds,
for garnish

Duck

2 Tbsp extra virgin olive oil
4 duck breasts

Broccolini

½ lb broccolini
¼ cup water
¼ cup lime juice
(from 2–3 limes)
2 cloves garlic, minced
Chili flakes

The sauce in this recipe is rather addictive, so be sure to serve this with lots of bread and vegetables to let people savour every last drop. The richness of the duck is incredible alongside the sweet, tangy sauce and the fresh broccolini is a lovely accompaniment to balance it all out. Finding local fowl is fairly easy. Most local butcher shops carry farm-raised Vancouver Island duck, which is always tender and well marbled. (Note: If duck isn't available, chicken thighs work well.) —EL

To make the sauce, in a small bowl, whisk together the lime juice, soy sauce, honey, vinegar, and cornstarch until no lumps remain. Pour the liquid into a blender and add the tomato paste, garlic, ginger, and then the sesame oil. Slice the plums in half and discard the pits. Add the plums to the blender and blend until you have a smooth sauce. (A few lumps and bumps are okay at this stage.)

Place the sauce in a small saucepan and bring to a boil over medium-high heat. As soon as it reaches a boil, turn down the heat and let simmer until it has a thick consistency, about 10 minutes. (It should easily coat the back of a spoon.) Remove from the heat and set aside.

While the sauce is simmering, prepare the duck breasts. Heat the oil in a non-stick skillet or cast iron pan over medium-high heat. Sear the duck breasts, one or two at a time so as not to crowd the pan, for 2 minutes per side, allowing a little longer for the skin side. Turn down the heat to low, nestle all the duck breasts into the pan, pour the sauce overtop, and simmer for 5 minutes, just to allow the sauce to reduce further and the duck to cook through.

Meanwhile, wash and dry the broccolini and trim the stems. Bring the water, lime juice, and garlic to a boil in a shallow saucepan over medium-high heat. Blanch the broccolini in the boiling liquid, turning it with tongs occasionally to ensure even cooking, until bright green and just starting to soften but still quite firm, 2–3 minutes. Place on a serving platter, drizzle any remaining cooking liquid overtop, and sprinkle with chili flakes to taste.

Place the duck on individual serving plates, top with the sauce, and garnish with sesame seeds.

Serve immediately.

You can store all the components of this dish separately. The sauce will keep in an airtight container in the fridge for up to 2 weeks, the duck will keep in an airtight container in the fridge for up to 3 days, and the broccolini will keep in an airtight container in the fridge for up to 1 week.

Herbs de Comox Valley Crusted Beef Tenderloin
with Foch Reduction

SERVES 4–6

Tenderloin

3 lb beef tenderloin roast,
    trimmed

1 tsp coarse sea salt

1 tsp cracked black pepper

½ cup extra virgin olive oil,
    divided

4 cloves garlic, minced

1 shallot, minced

¼ cup Herbes de Comox
    Valley

3 bay leaves

¼ cup tahini

Reduction

1 cup red wine

½ cup beef stock

¼ cup balsamic vinegar

2 tsp whole black
    peppercorns

1 tsp fine sea salt

2 Tbsp unsalted butter

Dried lavender buds,
    for garnish

---

*If you can't get ahold of Herbs
de Comox Valley, mix together
2 Tbsp fresh chopped oregano,
2 Tbsp thyme leaves, 1 Tbsp
fresh chopped savoury, 1 tsp
fresh chopped sage, 1 tsp fresh
chopped rosemary, 1 Tbsp dried
lavender buds.*

Perfect for Sunday dinners, casual summer outdoor dinners, and even more formal Christmas events, tenderloin is the epitome of versatility. Herb de Comox Valley is the Island's version of a traditional Herbes de Provence spice blend, available from Clever Crow Herbs and Spices. Tahini might seem like an odd choice, but it's the perfect consistency to ensure the herbs stick well to the seared roast, and it adds a lovely creamy nuttiness. I like to use Emandare Vineyard's Marechal-Cabernet Foch, a local red wine with deep fruity and earthy notes, for the reduction. —EL

To prepare the beef, pat it dry. If it is uneven in diameter, fold the tail end under so the meat is an even thickness along its length and tie together with butchers' twine, spacing the lines of twine about 1 inch apart along the length of the roast. Season with the salt and pepper.

Place ¼ cup of the oil in a small bowl or liquid measure. Add the garlic, shallot, and then the Herbes de Comox Valley. Mix well to combine and make a thick, herby paste. Set aside.

Preheat the oven to 325°F. Line a rimmed baking sheet with parchment paper.

Place the remaining ¼ cup of oil in a skillet over high heat. Sear the meat until caramelized, 2–3 minutes per side. Place the three bay leaves, parallel to each other and evenly spaced, along the centre of the prepared baking sheet. Place the meat on top and let rest for 2–3 minutes.

Using a pastry brush, coat the beef completely, including the underside, with the tahini, then pack the herb paste onto the beef so that it sticks to the tahini, making a thick crust.

Bake, uncovered, for 35–40 minutes, until the internal temperature measures 130°F for rare, 145°F for medium, and 160°F for well done. The roast will continue to cook after it has been removed from the oven, so let it rest for 10 minutes before carving and serving.

While the roast is cooking, prepare the reduction.

Place the wine, stock, balsamic, and peppercorns in a small saucepan and bring to a boil over medium-high heat. Turn down the heat to medium and simmer until it has reduced by half. Add the salt, continuing to reduce until syrupy, 2–3 minutes. Remove from the heat and allow to cool for 1 minute, then whisk in the butter to make a thick, glossy reduction.

To serve, slice the tenderloin into ½-inch-thick slices, sprinkle with lavender buds, and drizzle with the reduction.

The roast and reduction will keep in separate airtight containers in the fridge for up to 1 week.

Island Beef Brisket
Braised with Craft Beer and Coffee

SERVES 4–6

4 lbs beef brisket

½ cup plus 3 Tbsp extra virgin olive oil

1 Tbsp fine sea salt

Coarsely ground black pepper

½ cup finely ground dark coffee beans

3 large carrots, peeled and cut into chunks

2 celery stalks, cut into chunks

1 cooking onion, halved

3 cups craft-style beer

1 whole garlic bulb, unpeeled, cut in half cross-wise

1 (28 oz/796 ml) can diced tomatoes

1 bay leaf

2 Tbsp fresh thyme leaves

½ cup chopped fresh flat-leaf parsley

Coffee and beer are a wonderful flavour combination, especially when paired with a slow-braised piece of meat. I really like Vancouver Island Brewing's Sea Dog Amber Ale and a dark espresso bean from Royston Roasting Co. for this recipe. —DLA

Preheat the oven to 325°F.

Rub the brisket on all sides with the 3 Tbsp of oil and season with salt and pepper. Rub the finely ground coffee into the meat and set aside to rest.

Heat a large Dutch oven over medium-high heat and add the remaining ½ cup of oil. When the oil is hot, sear the meat on all sides until a crust has formed. Remove the meat from the pan and set aside. Place the cut carrots, celery, and onions in the pan (no need to wipe it out first) and sauté for 5–7 minutes, or until the vegetables begin to soften. Add the beer and deglaze the pan, using a wooden spoon to scrape up any bits from the bottom. Add the garlic, tomatoes with their juice, bay leaf, and thyme. Add the brisket, cover, and roast for 3 hours, or until fork-tender.

Once the brisket is cooked, lay it on a cutting board and let rest for 15 minutes. Strain out the vegetables from the juices and discard. Pour off some of the excess fat and then boil the remaining liquid on high heat until reduced by half, about 10 minutes. Slice the brisket across the grain, sprinkle parsley overtop, and serve with the reduced pan juices.

Leftovers will keep in an airtight container in the fridge for up to 5 days.

farm

farm

Espresso-Braised Beef Short Ribs
with Roasted Garlic Rosemary Mash

SERVES 4

Ribs

8–10 (each 3–4 inches)
  short ribs

2 tsp coarse sea salt

1 tsp cracked black pepper

2 Tbsp very finely ground
  espresso beans

4 Tbsp extra virgin olive
  oil, divided

1 large cooking onion

6 cloves garlic

1 cup freshly brewed
  espresso

¼ cup aged balsamic
  vinegar

1 (28 oz/796 ml) can
  whole tomatoes

2 cups beef stock

4 sprigs thyme

2 sprigs rosemary

1 bay leaf

Mash

1 unpeeled garlic bulb

2 Tbsp extra virgin olive oil

4 large potatoes (Yukon
  gold or other waxy
  variety)

¼ cup whipping (35%)
  cream

2 Tbsp cream cheese,
  cubed

¼ cup plus 1 Tbsp chilled,
  salted butter, cubed

½ tsp fine sea salt

1 sprig of rosemary (about
  1 Tbsp finely chopped
  leaves)

Short ribs are one of those easy company meals that can only appear to go wrong. Guests have often commented to me, "Oh no! The meat is falling off the bone!" In this case, that's the best outcome. It means the meat is tender and juicy. Short ribs may not look very elegant, but that is absolutely cancelled out by how tasty they are. Thanks to the espresso, the complexity of the sauce is almost as delicious as the meat itself. Try to find freshly roasted beans from a local roastery and use twice as much coffee as you would use for a cup of espresso to drink. This deepens the flavour even more and brings out the deep chocolate and fruity notes from the coffee into the braise itself. Add the hearty, herby mash and a simple, classic comfort-focused meal is born. (Note: You can cook these in a slow cooker for 6–8 hours on low and 4–6 hours on high.) —EL

To prepare the short ribs, rinse the ribs, pat dry, and set aside.

In a small dish, mix the salt and pepper with the ground coffee. Gently rub this coffee seasoning all over the short ribs.

In a heavy-bottomed skillet or Dutch oven, heat 2 Tbsp of the oil over medium-high heat. Sear the short ribs on all sides, working in batches so you don't overcrowd the pan. Take your time so the ribs are crisp on all sides. Set the seared ribs aside.

Preheat the oven to 375°F.

Roughly chop the onion and smash the garlic cloves.

In the same pan you used for the ribs, heat the remaining 2 Tbsp oil over medium-high heat and sauté the onion and garlic for 4–5 minutes. Scrape any bits from the bottom of the pan and then sauté for another 3–4 minutes, until the vegetables are starting to brown. Pour in the espresso and balsamic. Bring to a boil and let reduce for 2 minutes. Gently pour in the juice from the tomatoes and increase the heat to medium high. Add the tomatoes, crushing them in your hand as you do so.

Arrange the short ribs in the Dutch oven (or a roasting pan, if you prefer), tucking them close together. Pour the sauce over them and top with enough beef stock to cover them completely. Place the thyme, rosemary, and bay leaf in the pan and cover. Roast for 90 minutes, or until tender.

While the ribs are cooking, prepare the potatoes.

Cut the top of the head of garlic just enough to expose the cloves. Drizzle the cloves with the oil and place on some aluminum foil. Wrap the garlic tightly and place in the oven alongside the ribs.

Roast the garlic for 18 minutes, until tender and soft.

Bring a large saucepan of heavily salted water to a boil over high heat. Peel the potatoes and chop them into 1-inch cubes. Boil the potatoes until

(Continued on page 137)

(Continued from page 134)

tender, 7–10 minutes. Drain and place them in a large mixing bowl. Add the cream, cream cheese, the ¼ cup of butter, salt, and rosemary, then squish the roasted garlic out of the clove and add it to the bowl. Using an electric mixer, whip the potatoes until completely smooth.

To serve, discard the spices from the ribs. Remove the ribs from the braise and place them on a serving platter. Place the potatoes alongside them and top with the remaining 1 Tbsp butter. If you're plating the dish, place a spoonful of mashed potatoes on the plate, put a short rib in the centre, and drizzle with a little bit of braise for garnish.

You can store the potatoes in the fridge in an airtight container for up to 1 week, and the meat in a separate airtight container for up to 3 days.

Porterhouse Steaks
with Carrot Top Chimichurri

SERVES 4

Chimichurri
½ cup extra virgin olive oil
2 Tbsp apple cider vinegar
1 cup finely chopped fresh
   carrot fronds
3–4 cloves garlic, minced
¼ cup finely chopped mint
   leaves
1 tsp flaked sea salt
Cracked black pepper
1–2 tsp chili flakes
   (optional)

Marinade
½ cup extra virgin olive oil
⅓ cup coconut aminos
2 Tbsp lemon juice
2 cloves garlic, minced
1 tsp dried thyme
1 tsp dried rosemary
1 tsp dried oregano
1 tsp cracked black pepper

Steaks
4 (each 1-inch thick) bone-
   in porterhouse steaks
Flaked sea salt, for serving

There is nothing better than a gorgeous grass-fed Comox Valley steak grilled to perfection, except perhaps one topped with this deeply satisfying and easy-to-make sauce. I decided to try making this with the fresh green fronds from our CSA carrots instead of parsley as it seemed a shame to snap all that goodness off and just toss it in the compost. The results were earthy and delicious.—DLA

To make the chimichurri, place the oil and vinegar in a bowl and add the carrot fronds, garlic, mint, chili flakes (if using), salt, a pinch of pepper, and chili flakes (if using). Stir to combine. Let sit for at least 1 hour to release all of the flavours into the oil.

To prepare the steaks, combine the marinade ingredients in a large casserole dish. Add the steaks and coat thoroughly. Cover and marinate the steaks in the refrigerator overnight, being sure to flip them a few times to let the marinade soak in.

Remove the steaks from the fridge at least 30 minutes before you're ready to cook them. Heat a grill or cast-iron pan to medium-high heat. Grill or fry the steaks to your preferred doneness. Remove from the heat and let rest for at least 5 minutes.

Serve with a light sprinkling of salt and a generous dollop of chimichurri.

farm

Dark Chocolate Blackcurrant Swirl Ice Cream

MAKES 2 QUARTS
(ONE 9- X 5-INCH
LOAF PAN)

3 cups whipping (35%)
cream, divided
8 oz dark chocolate
(at least 65% cocoa),
chopped
1 cup granulated sugar
4 egg yolks
½ cup blueberry or
cranberry juice
2 tsp cornstarch
1 cup blackcurrants
1 tsp ground nutmeg
½ tsp ground cinnamon

Lovely velvety chocolate ice cream swirled with rich, spicy local black-currants is a tasty way to preserve these berries since their season is so short. When I'm making ice cream, I always over-spice as the spices' flavours are muted when frozen. (Note: You'll need an ice cream maker for this recipe.) —EL

Prepare your ice cream maker as per the manufacturer's instructions.

In a small saucepan, heat 1 cup of the cream over medium-low heat until it's just warm. Add the chocolate, remove from heat, let sit 3 minutes, then whisk until fully incorporated.

In a saucepan over medium heat, warm the remaining 2 cups of cream. In a mixing bowl, whisk together the sugar and yolks until light and fluffy. When the cream is warm, pour 1 cup in the mixing bowl and whisk it into the yolk mixture. Add another ½ cup of cream, whisking again, then pour the yolk-cream mixture into the pan with the remaining cream, and return to medium heat. Stir until thick enough to coat a spoon, 5 minutes. Remove from the heat and whisk in the cream-chocolate mix. Pour into a bowl, cover with plastic wrap, pressing down on the surface of the mixture, and refrigerate to cool and thicken until ready to churn the ice cream.

In a small saucepan, whisk the juice with the cornstarch until lump-free. Stir in the blackcurrants. Place over medium-high heat and add the nutmeg and cinnamon. Stirring constantly, bring the mixture to a rolling boil and boil for 1 minute. The sauce will be translucent. Remove from the heat, transfer to a bowl, and refrigerate, uncovered.

Follow the manufacturer's instructions to churn the ice cream.

Remove the sauce from the fridge and stir once.

Spoon one-third of the chocolate mixture into an ungreased 9- × 5-inch loaf pan, add half the sauce, and repeat. Using a spatula, fold the mixture twice to create a swirl. Place in the freezer, uncovered, and freeze until solid, 6–8 hours.

This will keep in an airtight container in the freezer for up to 3 months.

farm

Raspberry-Swirled Creamy Meringues

MAKES 1 DOZEN

Raspberry syrup
⅓ cup granulated sugar
½ pint fresh raspberries

Meringues
⅔ cup granulated sugar
2½ tsp cornstarch
1 tsp cream of tartar
¼ tsp fine sea salt
4 egg whites, room
　temperature

These meringues are like edible raspberry clouds—fluffy, crisp, and raspberry-tart. Meringues can be tricky, but I like to think that using farm-fresh free-range eggs, like those from Lockwood Farms in Cobble Hill, makes the whole process a whole lot better all round. —EL

Place ⅓ cup of sugar and the raspberries in a medium saucepan. Squish the berries to release the juices. Place over medium heat, stirring occasionally for about 3 minutes, until the sugar has dissolved. Let cool. Pour the raspberries through a fine-mesh strainer into a bowl. Discard the pulp and put the bowl of juice, uncovered, in the fridge. You'll have about ½ cup of syrup.

In a bowl, whisk together ⅔ cup of sugar, the cornstarch, cream of tartar, and salt.

In a separate bowl, using a stand mixer or hand-held beaters, beat the egg whites, starting on low speed and slowly increasing to medium-high. When peaks start to form, slowly pour in the sugar and cornstarch mixture as you continue to beat. After all the sugar mixture is added, increase the speed to high and whip for 2–3 minutes. Squish some meringue between your fingers. If it feels grainy, it's not quite ready. Beat for 1 minute more at a time, checking after each minute. When the sugar has dissolved, the mixture will feel smooth and have stiff glossy peaks. With the mixer running on low, slowly add half the syrup. Beat until incorporated.

Preheat the oven to 300°F (275°F in a hot dry climate or summer). Line a baking sheet with parchment paper.

Spoon tennis ball–sized dollops of meringue onto the parchment, 1 inch apart.

With a fork, gently swirl reserved syrup around each meringue.

Bake for 35 minutes, until puffed, just golden on top, and slightly cracked. Turn the oven off and leave the meringues there for 15 minutes. Crack the door open 2–3 inches and let sit for 25 minutes. Transfer to a wire rack and let cool to room temperature.

These will keep in an airtight container at room temperature for up to 3 days, or in the freezer for up to 2 months.

farm

Buffalo Milk Ice Cream
with Fresh Fruit and Herb Compote

SERVES 4

Ice cream
4 cups buffalo milk yogurt
¼ cup liquid honey
1 tsp pure vanilla extract
2 Tbsp lemon juice
Fine sea salt

Compote
2 cups fruit (apples and
 rhubarb should be
 cubed, cherries can
 be pitted and then left
 whole)
¼ cup liquid honey
1 Tbsp freshly squeezed
 lemon juice
¼ cup finely chopped
 herbs

SOME OF MY FAVOURITE
FLAVOUR COMBOS FOR
THE COMPOTE ARE:

Sour cherry and sage
Apple and rosemary
Rhubarb and fennel top
Kiwi and spearmint

When I was a child, we would take the long drive from Nanaimo to Deep Bay every weekend. I always got excited when I saw the sign for Parksville come into view. It meant one thing: The Dairy Queen was just around the corner. This is my grown-up version of the sundaes I loved then, and my children love these too! Buffalo milk yogurt is incredibly creamy, almost silky, and gives a gorgeous smoothness and deeply rich flavour to the ice cream. For the compote, I have given basic proportions that can be applied to any fruit and herb combination, so feel free to experiment to create your own! (Note: You'll need an ice cream maker for this recipe.) —DLA

Prepare your ice cream maker as per the manufacturer's instructions.

To make the ice cream, in a medium bowl, whisk together the yogurt, honey, vanilla, lemon juice, and a pinch of salt until the honey has fully dissolved. Pour the mixture into your ice cream mixer.

Follow the manufacturer's instructions to churn the ice cream. Place in an airtight container in the freezer for at least 3–4 hours, or preferably overnight. Frozen yogurt is best eaten within a month of freezing.

To make the compote, in a heavy-bottomed saucepan and over medium heat, mix together the fruit, honey, lemon juice, and herbs, stirring constantly until the honey has dissolved and the fruit is just starting to break down. The compote should be syrupy and chunky. It's not a purée.

Let cool to at least room temperature before serving on top of ice cream, about 1 hour.

This will keep in an airtight container in the fridge for up to 1 week.

farm

Black Tea Ice Cream

**MAKES ENOUGH ICE
CREAM TO FILL ONE
5- X 9- INCH LOAF PAN**

2 Tbsp black tea leaves
3 cups whipping (35%)
  cream
1 cup granulated sugar
6 egg yolks
2 tsp pure vanilla extract

Born out of a passion and love for tea, Westholme Tea Farm in Duncan is the home of tea culture in Canada. Owners Margit and Victor grow, harvest, and make tea on this wonderful 11-acre farm. Black tea is oxidized and bruised or kneaded to coax out its flavours. My favourite for this ice cream is their maple smoked black tea, but really any black tea will make this delicious. —EL

Prepare your ice cream maker as per the manufacturer's instructions.

Place the tea in a small bowl and pour in ¾ cup of boiling water. Let steep until you have an extra-concentrated brew.

In a small saucepan over medium heat, warm the cream. In a mixing bowl, whisk together the sugar and yolks until light and fluffy. When the cream is warm, whisk 1 cup of it into the yolk mixture. Whisk in another ½ cup and then pour the yolk-cream mixture into the saucepan with the remaining cream and return to medium heat.

Strain the tea, discard the tea leaves, and, stirring constantly, pour the tea into the cream mixture, along with the vanilla. Continue to stir for 4–5 minutes, until the mixture is thick enough to coat the back of a spoon.

Remove from the heat and pour through a fine-mesh strainer into a mixing bowl. Cover the bowl with plastic wrap, ensuring it touches the liquid to prevent a skin from forming. Refrigerate to chill completely, 4–6 hours or overnight.

Remove from the fridge, uncover, and stir. Pour this base into your ice cream maker. Follow the manufacturer's instructions to churn the ice cream. Spoon the ice cream into a 9- × 5-inch loaf pan and place in the freezer to chill completely, 2–3 hours.

This will keep, covered, in the freezer for up to 3 months.

Honey Mead Summer Spritzer

SERVES 1

Ice cubes
4 oz mead
1 wedge lime
8 oz soda or sparkling
   water
1 round lime slice

I was first introduced to mead through my husband, who has a doctorate in medieval studies. It is one of the oldest known alcoholic beverages and comes in a wide variety of forms, from a sparkling beer-like draft to a soft honey-scented wine. It also comes in a variety of flavours, depending on what extras are included in the fermentation process. I particularly like the Spiced Marionberry Melomel from Tugwell Creek Honey Farm and Meadery in Sooke. This recipe is much like a classic wine spritzer and is now our go-to for summer sippers. If you want to make a pitcher to serve a crowd, simply multiply all the ingredients by 10. —DLA

Fill a tall glass with ice cubes and pour the mead overtop. Add a squeeze of lime from the lime wedge and top with soda water. Stir well and garnish with the lime slice.

Goat Milk Lemon Verbena Panna Cotta
with Rhubarb Confit and Honeycomb

SERVES 4

Panna cotta
2 cups whole goat milk
½ cup honey
½-inch piece of ginger
    (peeled but left whole)
10 large lemon verbena
    leaves, plus extra for
    garnish
1 Tbsp unflavoured gelatin
¼ cup cold water

Compote
¼ cup honey
2 Tbsp lemon juice
2 cups chopped rhubarb
4-inch square of
    honeycomb, crumbled

Goat milk can be a funny thing—sometimes it's a little sour, other times it's sweet as anything. Taste it before using it so you can alter the sweetness in a recipe accordingly. Many goat dairies are popping up on Vancouver Island and selling milk instead of just using it for cheese. It contains fewer allergens and is almost completely lactose-free. (Note: If you can't get goat milk, whole cow milk is equally good.) —EL

In a large saucepan over medium-high heat, bring the milk to a simmer. Add the honey, ginger, and lemon verbena leaves. Stir to combine until the honey is melted. Bring just to a boil and remove from the heat. Let steep, uncovered, for 15 minutes, then discard the ginger and lemon verbena leaves.

While the milk is steeping, place the gelatin in a medium-sized liquid measuring cup and pour the cold water overtop. Mix slightly to combine and ensure the gelatin is wet and can dissolve. Set aside to bloom, about 5 minutes.

Pour the warm milk mixture over the gelatin and then whisk it in to remove any lumps.

Divide the warm goat milk mixture evenly between four ½-cup ramekins, small mason jars, or molds and refrigerate, uncovered, for 6 hours, or overnight, to set.

Preheat the oven to 325°F. Line a rimmed baking sheet with parchment paper.

In a mixing bowl, whisk together the honey and lemon juice, add the rhubarb, and toss to coat. Place on the prepared baking sheet in an even layer. Scrape out the bowl to get every last drop of honey mixture.

Bake for 20 minutes. Using a spatula, turn the rhubarb over and bake for another 15 minutes. It will be soft, golden, and caramelized. Carefully transfer the warm rhubarb and any juices that have pooled on the parchment paper to a small mixing bowl. Using a fork, break up the rhubarb until you have a smooth, thick mixture. Cover and refrigerate until needed.

To serve, set the ramekins of panna cotta in a shallow bowl of hot tap water for 10 seconds, ensuring no water spills into the ramekins. Remove from the water, place a small dish over the top of each ramekin, and flip them over to turn the panna cotta out onto the plates. Spoon the compote overtop and garnish with a piece of honeycomb and some lemon verbena leaves. Or spoon compote overtop the panna cotta in its dish.

The panna cotta and compote will keep in separate airtight containers in the fridge for up to 1 week.

farm

Sidney Spiced Spirit and Homemade Eggnog

SERVES 8

¼ cup granulated sugar
¼ cup pure maple syrup
2 strips orange peel
6 black peppercorns
4 cloves
3 star anise
2 cinnamon sticks
1 cup whipping (35%)
  cream
4 eggs, separated
2 cups whole milk
1 cup Sidney Spiced Spirit
Grated nutmeg, for garnish

Creamy and rich, this spiced eggnog is the perfect holiday drink. Making the spiced syrup first and then tempering the yolks ensures a consistently creamy and delicious flavour from first sip to the very last drip. Whipping the egg whites and folding them in keeps the drink light, despite the cream. Sidney Spiced Spirit is a locally distilled rum from Victoria Distillers, filled with spices of orange peel, vanilla bean, ginger, and star anise. It is warm, complex—and perfect in this recipe. (Note: You can also use dark rum or bourbon.) —EL

In a small saucepan over medium heat, place the sugar, maple syrup, and ½ cup of water. Stir to combine, then add the orange peel, peppercorns, cloves, star anise, and cinnamon sticks. Turn down the heat to low and let simmer gently for 20 minutes, without touching it, until the sugar has dissolved and the spices have fully infused the syrup. Remove from the heat and strain through a fine-mesh sieve into a large mixing bowl, discarding the spices.

While the syrup is infusing, using a hand-held or stand mixer, whip the cream to soft peaks. In a separate bowl, beat the egg whites to stiff peaks. Gently fold the cream and meringue together and refrigerate, covered.

In a large saucepan over medium heat, bring the milk to a simmer.

Add the egg yolks to the spiced syrup. Whisk until light and fluffy. Pour a ladle of warm milk into the yolks and syrup mixture and whisk to combine. Repeat with another ladle of warm milk, then pour the yolk, syrup, and milk mixture into the saucepan with the remaining milk. Bring back to a simmer over medium heat, stirring constantly for 1 minute. Remove from the heat, transfer to a bowl, and refrigerate, covered.

When ready to serve, add the spirit to the eggnog and fold in the meringue cream mixture. Ladle into glasses and serve over ice with a dusting of freshly grated nutmeg.

est

forest

When I close my eyes and stand very still, I can smell the forest floor. It is the scent of sweet cedar bark warmed by the sun, of overripe fruit hanging too long on the trees, of the cool earth, and the darkness of tree roots. This is the fragrance of my childhood, and it always makes me hungry.

Spending my early summers on the Gulf Islands, I was immersed in the wild foods that were all around us, and to this very day they are still my go-to when I want to create something to share with guests, something that will give them a true taste of here. These are the foods we harvest ourselves: the berries, picked under hot summer skies, that become pies and crumbles; the mint that grows with fervor along the edges of yards, adding a fresh little twist to cocktails; the wild, earthy mushrooms that make simple pasta bakes extra special.

In the forest, you'll find wild plums and figs growing in harmony with plumes of lavender and lemon balm. Several varieties of blackberries spread their brambles along the dark edges of deep forests; wild onion, ginger, and other assorted herbs and spices grow prolifically across the Island's floor.

Of course, foraging should always be done with a measure of caution and, for the novice, under the supervision of a field expert. Oftentimes, berries found at a farmers market can look very similar to some in the wild that are inedible and, in extreme cases, poisonous. Likewise, the fungi family can vary enormously, so you should always be completely certain that the mushrooms you're adding to your recipe are safe to eat.

For the hunters among us, wild game in the forms of venison, rabbit, and even boar roam alongside trees of elder, lilac, and nut-bearing walnut, hazel, and oak. And, if we're talking about hunting, I must reaffirm that good hunting practices include holding a certified licence for gun use and following legislated dates for open hunting and trapping seasons. Also, it's important that we remember that harvesting outside of provincial parameters is considered poaching and is a serious and dangerous offence.

This chapter is a celebration of all those delicacies the Island proffers: the huckleberries and salal that grow from the stumps of fallen giants throughout the forest floors; the rosehips and blackberries that line the roads and beachside up and down the Island; the elusive and hidden truffles and mushrooms that are the secret of foragers; and the inherited treasures of backyard crabapples, figs, and sour cherries. These flavours are crafted by nature to pair perfectly with the wild meats of rabbit, venison, and boar. So please forage safely, harvest responsibly, and hunt mindfully. —DLA

forest

forest

Sautéed Chanterelles
with Black Garlic

SERVES 4 AS A SIDE

1 lb fresh chanterelle
  mushrooms
1 bulb black garlic
3 Tbsp salted butter
¼ cup dry white wine
Coarse sea salt and ground
  black pepper
Curly-leaf parsley, for
  garnish

There is something so simple about allowing ingredients to speak for themselves. Chanterelles are ideal for doing just that. Often found on roadside stands and at farmers markets at the end of August, these beauties don't need any extra attention, just a little love. Black garlic is regular garlic that has gone through a long, slow fermentation process, so it tastes like roasted garlic. It has even more health benefits than regular garlic—and it tastes delicious! Pair these with fresh pasta for an easy yet sophisticated dinner.—EL

Wash the mushrooms carefully and remove any bits of dirt. Pat dry and slice in half. Separate the cloves from the bulb of garlic and remove the skins. Crush each clove with the back of a knife to squish it, keeping it whole, and set aside.

In a medium saucepan over medium heat, melt the butter. When it begins to bubble, add the garlic, swirling the pan to gently move it around. Add the chanterelles and toss to coat in the butter. Sauté for 1–2 minutes, then pour in the wine. Sauté until almost all the liquid has evaporated, 5–10 minutes, turning the mushrooms frequently to ensure even cooking.

Transfer to a serving platter, season to taste with salt and pepper, and garnish with parsley.

These will keep in an airtight container in the fridge for up to 3 days.

forest

Cream of Lovage Soup
with Edible Spring Herb Flowers

SERVES 4–6

2 Tbsp salted butter

1 medium cooking onion, finely chopped

2 cups loosely packed, chopped fresh lovage leaves

8 cups chicken stock

4 medium Yukon gold potatoes, peeled and cut into 1-inch cubes

Coarse sea salt and cracked black pepper

Small handful fresh spring herb flowers

2 Tbsp hemp or good quality olive oil

Lovage is one of the first herbs to come into full bloom in our garden, and its presence hints at the glorious bounty that is to come in the following months. It's also the first real taste of green that we get after the long, dark West Coast winter, and so I eat it with and in everything I can! If you've never tried lovage, it has a similar flavour to celery but it's slightly stronger and a bit more savoury. This soup is probably my favourite lovage dish, as the full flavour comes through and stands proud in all its deliciousness. I like to top the soup with the fresh flowers that bloom on my herbs around the same time the lovage appears—any variety you have on hand will do. —DLA

In a large stockpot or Dutch oven over medium heat, melt the butter. Add the chopped onions and sauté for 4–5 minutes, or until slightly translucent. Add the lovage and sauté until it wilts, 1–2 minutes. Add the chicken stock and potatoes and increase the heat to medium-high. Bring to a boil for 15–20 minutes, or until the potatoes are soft and break apart easily with a fork. Remove from the heat and let cool completely.

Once the soup is completely cool, working in batches, purée the soup in a blender until smooth. Return to the pot and warm through over medium heat. Season to taste with salt and pepper, and drizzle with hemp or olive oil. Serve garnished with fresh herb flower blossoms. I love rosemary and sweet cicely, but experiment with your own favourites.

forest

Wild Mushroom Veggie Burgers
with Creamy Blue Cheese Dressing

SERVES 6

Patties

1 lb wild mushrooms
  (shiitake, portabella,
  oyster all work well)
1 tsp fine sea salt
1 (14 oz) can black beans,
  drained and rinsed
1 red onion
2 garlic cloves
4 Tbsp extra virgin
  olive oil, divided
¼ cup rolled oats
1 egg
2 Tbsp Dijon mustard
1 tsp chili powder
1 tsp ground cumin
½ tsp smoked paprika

Dressing

½ cup full-fat Greek yogurt
¼ cup full-fat mayonnaise
1 Tbsp red wine vinegar
2 tsp Worcestershire sauce
1 garlic clove
½ tsp fine sea salt
½ tsp ground black pepper
1 cup crumbled blue
  cheese

Assembly

6 hamburger buns
12 slices lettuce
1 tomato, sliced
3 pickles, sliced

Veggie burgers are finicky and have a tendency to fall apart, taste bland, and be not at all meat-like. This burger is not like those. I've developed a few tricks to produce veggie burgers that never fail to please my veggie-loving friends. Using fresh mushrooms and hand-rolled local oats makes them even yummier. —EL

Preheat the oven to 375°F. Place one rack in the top third of the oven and one in the bottom third. Line three rimmed baking sheets with parchment paper.

To make the patties, chop the mushrooms. Spread them in an even layer on one baking sheet and sprinkle the salt overtop. Spread the black beans in an even layer on the second baking sheet.

Place both baking sheets in the oven (I usually put the beans on the top and the mushrooms on the bottom) and roast for 15 minutes. Remove from the oven, drain off any liquid that has collected on the mushroom baking sheet, and let the mushrooms and black beans cool. Leave the oven on.

Roughly chop the onion and garlic, and sauté in 2 Tbsp of the oil in a skillet over medium heat for 4–5 minutes, until very soft and well caramelized. Transfer to a blender.

Roughly chop the oats and add to the blender along with the egg, Dijon, chili powder, cumin, and paprika. Pulse once or twice to mix then add the black beans and blend to form a thick, creamy paste. Transfer to a mixing bowl.

Place the mushrooms in the blender—no need to wipe it out—and pulse to chop them into small pieces. Add them to the black bean mixture and mix well.

Scoop the mixture into six patties, about ¾-inch thick, onto the third prepared baking sheet, and spread them a bit with a spoon until they are in a flat patty shape. Drizzle the remaining 2 Tbsp olive oil overtop.

Bake for 15 minutes, rotate the pan 180 degrees, and bake for 10 minutes more.

While the burgers are in the oven, make the dressing. In a small bowl, whisk together the yogurt, mayo, vinegar, and Worcestershire sauce. Finely mince the garlic and whisk it in, along with the salt and pepper, until the dressing is completely lump-free. Stir in the blue cheese and set aside until you're ready to assemble the burgers.

Toast the buns, if you like, and assemble the burgers with a patty, lettuce, tomato, pickle, and, of course, a good few dollops of blue cheese dressing.

Patties will keep in an airtight container in the fridge for up to 2 days, or in the freezer for up to 3 months. Thaw completely before cooking. Cooked patties will keep in an airtight container in the fridge for up to 3 days. Reheat in the oven or a skillet. The dressing will keep in an airtight container in the fridge for up to 1 week.

Edible Mushrooms of Vancouver Island

We admit we're spoiled when it comes to wild mushrooms here on the Island, but that's not surprising given that we live in a temperate rainforest and mushrooms love damp, wet places. This list is in no way comprehensive; these are simply a few of the more well-known and best-loved varieties that are readily available in the wild or through professional foragers. There are several good books and references for identifying foraged mushrooms, but if you are a novice, please don't pick and eat without the guidance of an experienced guide. —DLA

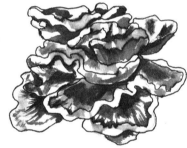

Chanterelles
Cantharellus cibarius
FEATURES: dense and meaty with a hint of slightly fruity flavours
FOUND: late summer into fall

Chicken of the Woods
Laetiporus sulphureus
FEATURES: chicken-like texture and flavour
FOUND: late spring, summer, and fall

Oyster Mushrooms
Panellus serotinus
FEATURES: delicate texture and mildly fruity flavour
FOUND: spring and fall

Lobster Mushrooms
Hypomyces lactifluorum
 FEATURES: firm dense texture
  with slightly seafood-like
  flavour
 FOUND: summer and fall

Matsutake (Pine)
Tricholoma magnivelare
 FEATURES: pungent, sweet,
  and spicy
 FOUND: fall

Black Morels
Morchella elata
 FEATURES: deep, earthy
  flavour
 FOUND: early spring

Porcini
Boletus edulis
 FEATURES: dense texture
  and earthy, nutty flavour
 FOUND: fall

Shaggy Manes
Coprinus comatus
 FEATURES: soft, white flesh
  with mild, earthy flavour
 FOUND: early spring and
  late fall

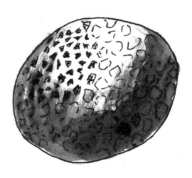

Western Giant Puffball
Lycoperdon perlatum
 FEATURES: firm, light flesh
  with mild flavour
 FOUND: spring, summer,
  and fall

forest

Truffle Pappardelle
with Parmadammer

SERVES 4

1 truffle
¾ cup warm water

Pasta
4 eggs
¼ cup extra virgin olive oil,
    plus extra for rubbing
1 tsp fine sea salt
2 cups all-purpose flour,
    plus extra for dusting

Sauce
1 clove garlic
2 Tbsp extra virgin olive oil
2 Tbsp truffle oil
1 egg
3 yolks
¾ cup grated
    Parmadammer or
    Parmesan cheese
Fine sea salt and ground
    black pepper

As you leaf through this book, it might seem that literally everything grows on this Island—and that includes truffles. Our local truffles are rich and earthy in flavour. They're most commonly found at the base of old Garry oak trees, but for best results, ask a forager at a local farmer's market. You're welcome to use an Italian or French truffle here if they are easier to come by. Parmadammer is made by Natural Pastures Cheese Company, a local cheese company. It's their version of Parmesan. Made with local milk, it's robust and full flavoured. —EL

First, clean the truffle. Hold it under cold, running water and, using a clean toothbrush, brush off any bits of dirt from the crevices.

Fill a small bowl with the warm water and submerge the truffle. Let it sit for about 30 minutes, or up to 6 hours, to let the flavour infuse.

In a medium bowl, whisk together the eggs, oil, and salt. Switch to a spatula or wooden spoon, and slowly begin to mix in the flour, ½ cup at a time, stirring after each addition until it comes together in a ball.

Sprinkle a little flour on the counter and knead the pasta dough with the heels of your hands, turning and folding as you go, for 8–10 minutes, until soft and silky. It should be sticky but soft.

Divide the dough into quarters and rub each one with a little oil to keep them moist. Using a rolling pin and well-floured work surface, roll the first quarter out to a 12- × 6-inch rectangle and sprinkle the surface lightly with flour.

Roll the dough through your pasta maker several times, making it one notch thinner than before each time, until it is two notches from as thin as it can be. Repeat with the remaining three pieces of pasta dough. (You can also roll it out by hand, if you like.) Using a pizza cutter, cut the long sheets in half widthwise and then into ¾- to 1-inch-wide strips. Toss the strips in flour, ensuring they are well coated, and let sit to dry slightly.

Bring a large saucepan of heavily salted water to a boil over high heat.

Finely mince the garlic. Put it in a large skillet and whisk in both oils. Add the egg and yolks and continue to whisk until light and fluffy. Place over low heat, continuing to whisk until thick and creamy, 5–8 minutes. Remove the truffle from its water and whisk the truffle water into the egg mixture. Whisk in the cheese to make a velvety-smooth sauce.

Place all the pasta in the boiling water and stir to avoid sticking. Boil, uncovered, for 4–5 minutes, until the pasta is cooked through. Remove from the pan and add to the sauce. Using tongs, toss the pasta in the sauce. Divide the pasta among the serving plates and, using a mandolin, shave the truffle over the pasta and season to taste with salt and pepper.

The cooked pasta, covered in its sauce, will keep in an airtight container in the fridge for up to 2 days.

Nettle and Chèvre Ravioli

SERVES 6

Pasta
6 large eggs
4 cups semolina flour
Fine sea salt

Filling
2 Tbsp extra virgin olive oil
1 shallot, finely minced
1 clove garlic, finely
    minced
8 cups loosely packed,
    washed spring nettle
    leaves
2 Tbsp water
¾ cup chèvre
½ cup grated Parmesan
    cheese
¼ cup panko bread crumbs
1 tsp dried chili flakes
½ tsp sea salt
½ tsp cracked black pepper
Flour for dusting
⅓ cup extra virgin olive oil
Flaked sea salt and cracked
    black pepper
Freshly grated Parmesan,
    for garnish

Nettles are one of those things that most people try desperately to avoid, but once you've actually eaten them, I'm sure you'll love them. They have a deeply green flavour to them, much like spinach but more so, and in most cases, the two can be interchanged. To get the best out of nettles, be sure to pick only the top new leaves that appear in the spring (the older leaves become bitter quickly) and wear gloves when picking to avoid being stung. Applying heat to nettles magically takes their sting out, making them palatable. —DLA

To make the pasta, place the eggs, flour, and salt in a food processor and pulse until the mixture comes together. Pour the contents out onto a lightly floured work surface and, using your hands, bring them together into a rough ball. Knead the ball with the heels of your hands, turning and folding as you go to develop the gluten in the flours. The dough is ready when it is soft and silky, about 10 minutes. Wrap it in plastic wrap and set aside in the fridge to rest for at least 30 minutes to overnight.

To make the filling, heat the oil in a large skillet over medium-high heat. Add the minced shallots and garlic and sauté until the shallots begin to become translucent, about 1 minute. Add the nettles and water and sauté for another 3–4 minutes, or until the water has evaporated and the greens are fully wilted and soft—they should shrink to slightly less than half their original bulk. Remove from the heat and let cool completely.

Place the cooled nettle mixture in a food processor and pulse until the greens are well chopped. Add the chèvre, Parmesan, panko, chili flakes, salt, and pepper and pulse a few more times to combine. Refrigerate, covered, until ready to use.

To make the ravioli, roll the dough through your pasta maker several times, making it one notch thinner than before each time, until it is thin enough to see through slightly but not so thin your fingers go through easily. If you don't have a pasta machine, you can roll the dough out with a rolling pin as well. You want long strips of dough, about 12 × 6 inches.

I use a ravioli press to make ravioli, and I highly recommend using one. Simply lay one sheet of pasta over the mold, place a teaspoon of the filling into each of the pockets, being sure to leave room around the edges, cover with another sheet of pasta, and then use a rolling pin to press the pasta sheets together and separate the ravioli.

Lightly toss the individual raviolo in flour and place them in a single layer on a baking sheet until ready to cook.

Bring a large saucepan of lightly salted water to a boil over high heat. Carefully drop all the ravioli into the water and boil for 6–7 minutes, or until al dente. Drain the pasta, toss with the olive oil, sprinkle with a pinch of salt and pepper, and top with freshly grated Parmesan. Serve immediately.

forest

Garlic Scape and Walnut Pesto Pasta

SERVES 4

(MAKES 2 CUPS PESTO)

¼ lb garlic scapes (about
  2 cups chopped)
1 cup extra virgin olive oil
2 Tbsp lemon juice
¾ cup walnut pieces
½ tsp chili flakes
½ tsp fine sea salt
¼ tsp cracked black pepper
1 cup grated Parmesan
  cheese, plus more for
  garnish
1 lb pasta, preferably
  linguini or fettuccini

When garlic scapes first turned up in my first CSA box, I had to ask the farmer what the swirly green stems were! They are incredibly tasty, with a mild yet noticeable garlic flavour. I love making them into a pesto. Once you've got the pesto made, you can whisk some into a salad dressing, or add it to some yogurt to create a delicious veggie dip. (Note: You won't use all the pesto for this recipe.)—EL

Wash and shake dry the scapes. Trim off the ends and chop into 1–2-inch long pieces. Place the scapes in a blender with ¼ cup water and pulse to mince. Add the oil and lemon juice, followed by the walnuts, chili flakes, salt, and pepper. Blend until you have a smooth, creamy paste. (A few lumps and bumps are okay.) Scrape down the sides of the bowl with a spatula, add the Parmesan, and blend until fully incorporated. Transfer to an airtight container and refrigerate until needed.

Cook the pasta according to the package directions. Drain the pasta, reserving about ¼ cup of the cooking water. Spoon ½ cup of the pesto over the pasta and add a few tablespoons of pasta water to thin it, if necessary. Toss the pasta well with the pesto to ensure the pasta is evenly coated. Feel free to add more pesto if you like your pasta extra saucy.

Garnish with some Parmesan, if you like, and serve immediately.

This pesto can be frozen in ice cube trays so you can enjoy it all year long. It also keeps in an airtight container in the fridge for up to 1 month.

Oyster Mushroom, Ricotta, and Blackened Chard Pasta Bake

1 lb oyster mushrooms
  (2–2½ cups peeled)
6 Swiss chard leaves
2 shallots
3 garlic cloves
¼ cup extra virgin olive oil
Coarse sea salt and ground
  black pepper, plus more
  for serving
2 Tbsp salted butter,
  plus more for greasing
  the pan
½ cup dry white wine
1 cup whipping (35%)
  cream
2 tsp chopped rosemary
  leaves
1 tsp thyme leaves,
  plus additional thyme
  for garnish
1 tsp chili flakes
1½ cups ricotta, divided
  (to make your own
  ricotta, see page 116)
1 lb fusilli, penne, or
  farfalle pasta

Oyster mushrooms are meaty and packed with flavour. Because of the way they grow, they easily pull apart into strips. I like to fry them before incorporating them into a dish. Crisp on the outside, juicy on the inside, they are a lovely substitute for tofu or meat. They can also be used as a crispy garnish, just like fried onions. Caramelizing the mushrooms and blackening the chard adds so much character to this simple dish. Delicious, healthy comfort food at its finest. (And leftovers make an amazing lunch!) —EL

Brush the mushrooms to remove any dirt. Working with one mushroom at a time, hold a mushroom in the centre between your thumb and index finger, with the stem pointing towards your wrist and your thumb on top. Use your other hand to carefully pull on the side of the mushroom so it separates all the way down to the stem, making a ¼- to ½-inch-wide peel or strip. It will be widest at the top and thinner at the bottom where it pulls off the stem. Continue until it has been completely peeled, and repeat with the rest of the mushrooms. They shrink quite a bit in the pan, so don't be alarmed when you see how much you start off with.

Roughly chop the Swiss chard stems into pieces, slice the leaves down the stem, and slice the leaves into ribbons. Chop the shallots and mince the garlic.

Heat the oil in a skillet over medium-high heat. Add one piece of mushroom. If it sizzles as soon as it hits the pan, add the rest of the mushrooms, shake the pan once to allow them to spread out evenly, and season to taste with salt and pepper. Let sear for 1–2 minutes without touching them. You want them to crisp up. When you see the edges starting to turn golden and curl, shake the pan and, using a wooden spoon, stir and rotate them so they don't stick and can caramelize on the other side. Sear for another 1–2 minutes, then remove them from the pan and set aside. Place the Swiss chard in the pan and place on medium heat. Sauté the chard until the stems are blackened and the leaves are wilted, 5–7 minutes. Add the chard to the mushrooms.

Place the shallots and garlic in the pan along with the butter. Sauté over medium heat for 2–3 minutes, until the shallots are just soft and the garlic is golden. Add the wine and deglaze the pan. When most of the wine has evaporated, add the cream, herbs, and chili flakes. Let simmer for 5 minutes to reduce slightly. Remove from the heat and stir in 1 cup of the ricotta.

Preheat the oven to 375°F. Grease a 13- × 9-inch baking dish.

Bring a large saucepan of salted water to a boil. Add the pasta and cook until just al dente, 1–2 minutes less than the package directions suggest. Drain the pasta, reserving ¼ cup of the pasta water, return to the pan, and add the cream sauce. Toss to coat completely and transfer to the prepared

baking dish. Top the pasta with the chard and mushrooms. Shake the dish
gently so the vegetables settle into the pasta. Dollop the remaining ½ cup of
ricotta overtop.

Bake for 18–20 minutes, until sauce is bubbling and the exposed pieces
of pasta are slightly golden. Serve with a sprinkle of salt and pepper and fresh
thyme on top.

This pasta will keep in an airtight container in the fridge for up to 5 days.

Ortega-Braised Chicken

with Wild Morels

SERVES 4

4 chicken quarters, skin on

2 Tbsp extra virgin olive oil

Coarse sea salt and cracked
 black pepper

1 cup all-purpose flour

¼ lb side bacon, cut into
 1-inch pieces

1 lb fresh morels

1 garlic clove

1 medium sweet onion,
 diced

2 Tbsp thyme leaves, plus
 a few sprigs to garnish

½ cup whipping (35%)
 cream

8 carrots, halved
 lengthwise and then cut
 into 3-inch pieces

3 cups Ortega white wine

Given its ability to withstand the relatively colder climate here on Vancouver Island, Ortega is one of our strongest local varietals of grapes grown for winemaking. I adore it as a drinking wine and really love to cook with it as much as I can. It is my go-to wine when I need a strong white to boost a dish. Here its sweetness complements the earthy morels and savoury meat. It's my favourite one-pot comfort food! —DLA

Separate the chicken quarters into drumsticks and thighs, or have your butcher do this for you.

In a large Dutch oven over medium-high heat, warm the oil. Season the chicken with salt and pepper. Dredge it in the flour and, working in batches, brown it on both sides in the warm oil. Set aside. Add the bacon to the pan (no need to wipe it out first) and cook until crisp. Set aside with the chicken.

Turn down the heat to medium and add the morels, garlic, onion, and thyme to the pan. Sauté until the mushrooms soften, the onion becomes translucent, and the garlic begins to caramelize, 6–7 minutes. Add the cream, stirring to combine, and then add the chicken, bacon, carrots, and wine. Cover and simmer on medium-low heat for 45 minutes. Remove the lid and let simmer for another 20 minutes.

Garnish each serving with thyme and serve with crusty bread.

Salal Berry-Glazed Venison Tenderloin

SERVES 6

Glaze
2 cups salal berries, rinsed
    and stems removed
2 Tbsp granulated sugar
1 Tbsp lemon juice
2 tsp grated lemon zest
1 Tbsp fresh rosemary
    leaves
2 Tbsp water
Fine sea salt

Venison
1½ lb venison loin
4 Tbsp extra virgin
    olive oil, divided
Flaked sea salt and cracked
    black pepper

Salal berries are reluctant to come off their stems and will simply burst apart if you try too hard to manhandle them. Instead, remove the entire berry stem from the plant, much like you would with grapes, and then place the bunches in the freezer overnight. Once frozen they'll come off easily and be ready for cooking. Look for them in late July and throughout August.

Salal berries are the unsung heroes of the foraging world. High in vitamin C and antioxidants, they're poised to be the next superfood once the world at large discovers them. Salal berries go really well with gamey meats like our local venison. If you're not a hunter, you'll find most of the great butchers here on Vancouver Island carry wild meats. —DLA

To make the glaze, place the berries, sugar, lemon juice and zest, rosemary, water, and a pinch of salt in a medium-sized heavy-bottomed saucepan over medium heat. Bring to a low boil (just a bit more than a simmer). Cook for 10 minutes, or until the berries begin to break down and the mixture is a deep purple. Remove from the heat and mash with a potato masher. Cook for another 5 minutes and then run the mixture through a food mill to remove any remaining solids. Set aside.

Preheat the oven to 400°F.

To prepare the venison, take it from the fridge at least 30 minutes before you plan to cook it to bring it to room temperature. Rub the entire loin with 2 Tbsp of the oil and then sprinkle liberally with salt and pepper.

Set a large cast iron, or other heavy ovenproof skillet, over high heat. When it's good and hot, add the remaining 2 Tbsp of oil. Sear the tenderloin on all sides to ensure a good, dark crust and then remove from the heat, leaving it in the pan. Using a barbecue brush, coat the meat with a good layer of the glaze and then place in the oven.

Cook for 5 minutes and then apply another coat of the glaze. Do this one more time. The internal temperature of the venison should show as 135°F on a meat thermometer. Venison should be cooked to medium-rare at the most; otherwise it can become tough and dry.

Remove the loin from the oven, transfer to a serving platter, and give it another coating of glaze. Let rest for at least 5 minutes before slicing.

Leftovers can be stored in an airtight container in the fridge for up to 1 week.

forest

Rabbit and Sour Cherry Ragout

SERVES 4

4–5 lb whole rabbit

2 tsp coarse sea salt

2 tsp cracked black pepper

¼ cup extra virgin olive oil

1 leek

1 large yellow zucchini or
  summer squash

2 cups halved radishes

2 cups pitted sour cherries

1 cup rosé wine

1 cup chicken stock

2 tsp fresh summer savoury

1 tsp marjoram leaves

4 thyme sprigs

1 bay leaf

1 cup garden peas

A ragout, different from an Italian-style ragú, is typically a stew of meat and vegetables, served alongside a starch. This summer version of the French comfort food is bright with sour cherries and fresh summer herbs and vegetables, and hearty, thanks to the rabbit. I love to pair this with the Truffle Pappardelle (page 174), Garlic Scape and Walnut Pesto Pasta (page 178), or Deep-Fried Zucchini Blossoms (page 64) for a true summer experience. (Note: If rabbit isn't available, use 2 lb of chicken thighs. If sour cherries are not available, use sweet cherries and switch out the rosé for a red wine.) —EL

Cut the rabbit into six pieces. Pat dry. Sprinkle with the salt and pepper and gently rub them into the meat.

In a skillet over medium-high heat, warm the oil. Working in batches so you don't crowd the pan, sear the rabbit pieces until well browned, 3–5 minutes per side. Put the meat on a plate and leave the drippings in the pan. Preheat the oven to 350°F.

Wash the leek and zucchini well. Slice the leek into thin rounds and the zucchini into ¼-inch-thick half-moons. Sauté the leek over medium heat in the drippings in the skillet until soft, about 3 minutes. Add the zucchini and radishes and sauté for 2–3 minutes, until lightly seared. Add the cherries, wine, and stock. Turn up the heat to high. As soon as it reaches a boil remove from the heat.

Place the rabbit pieces in a roasting pan just large enough to hold them without crowding, pour the sauce overtop, and sprinkle the herbs overtop. The sauce won't fully cover the meat. Cover tightly and roast for 1 hour.

Remove from the oven and let rest for 5 minutes to cool and set slightly. Remove and discard the herbs. Using two forks, pull the meat off the bones, shredding it directly in the roasting pan. Fold the peas into the meat.

Serve immediately. The peas will cook from the heat of the ragout and stay firm and bright.

This will keep in an airtight container in the fridge for up to 1 week.

forest

Huckleberry Hand Pies

2 cups huckleberries
2 Tbsp icing sugar
2 tsp cornstarch
2 Tbsp lemon juice
1 (14 oz/397 grams) box
   puff pastry dough,
   thawed
1 egg
1 Tbsp cold water
2 Tbsp coarse golden sugar

Huckleberries are one of my favourite summer treats. There's just something so delicious about strolling through a cool forest, hidden from the sun by the giant fir trees, and coming upon a bounty of bright pink, super-tart berries. They're not the easiest fruits to collect. In fact, some people even craft rakes to harvest them more easily. I prefer to pick them handful by handful and tuck them away in the freezer until I have a decent quantity. The problem is, I can never wait long enough to have enough for a full pie. Thus, the huckleberry hand pie was born. —DLA

Preheat the oven to 375°F. Line a baking sheet with parchment paper.

Place the huckleberries, sugar, and cornstarch in a mixing bowl and stir to combine. Add the lemon juice and let sit for 5 minutes to macerate.

Unwrap the pastry dough and lay the two sheets out on the prepared baking sheet. Cut each piece of pastry into four squares and place a heaping tablespoon or two of huckleberries right in the centre of each square. Lightly beat the egg and water together in a small bowl to make an egg wash and brush the edges of the squares with some of it. Fold over the pastry to enclose the pie filling pressing lightly to seal. Brush the tops of the pies lightly with the remaining egg wash and sprinkle with the golden sugar.

Bake for 20–25 minutes, or until the puff pastry is golden brown. Let cool on a wire rack for at least 10 minutes to ensure the filling is cool enough to eat.

These keep in an airtight container at room temperature for up to 3 days.

forest

Dad's Blackberry Apple Pie

SERVES 6–8

Pastry

¾ cup unsalted butter

3 cups all-purpose flour, plus additional flour for rolling out the pastry

1 Tbsp granulated sugar

1 tsp fine sea salt

⅓ cup very cold 100% vegetable shortening

½ cup ice water

Filling

¼ cup cold, unsalted butter

6 tart apples, peeled, cored, and sliced

2 cups fresh, sweet blackberries

½ cup plus 1 Tbsp packed golden sugar

3 Tbsp all-purpose flour

Ground cinnamon

Fine sea salt

1 egg

1 Tbsp water

Every summer when the blackberries are ripe, my dad sends us "kids" out to pick buckets of them while he collects apples from the trees. Watching him chop the apples, tuck in the pastry, and sprinkle the pies with sugar is one of my favourite things in life—second only to tucking into a warm slice straight from the oven. Dad loves his with classic vanilla ice cream, and I eat mine the English way, with a thick slice of extra-aged dry cheddar cheese. —DLA

To make the pastry, cut the butter into ½-inch cubes. Refrigerate until needed.

Place the flour, sugar, and salt in a food processor and pulse a few times to combine. Add all the butter and shortening. Pulse until you see pea-sized pieces of butter. With the machine running, slowly pour in the ice water and mix until the dough begins to form. Tip the pastry out onto a sheet of plastic wrap and, using the plastic wrap to help you, form a disc. Refrigerate for at least 30 minutes, or up to overnight.

Place the apple slices and blackberries in a large mixing bowl. Sprinkle the fruit with the ½ cup of sugar, the flour, and a pinch of cinnamon and salt. Stir gently to combine.

Preheat the oven to 425°F. Place a 9-inch deep-dish pie plate on a rimmed baking sheet.

When you're ready to bake, remove the pastry from the fridge and cut it in half. On a well-floured work surface, roll out each half to a 10 to 11-inch disc. Turn and flour the pastry as you roll so that it does not stick. Fold the pastry in half and then half again. This will help centre it when you place it on the pie plate.

Line the bottom of the pie plate with one pastry disc. Cut the butter into ½-inch cubes and set aside. Pour the fruit into the crust, mounding it slightly. Scatter cubes of butter over fruit before top pastry is added (it will melt into the pie). Cover with the other pastry disc and crimp the edges of the pastry together. Mix the egg with the 1 Tbsp water to make an egg wash. Brush the top of the pie with the egg wash and sprinkle the remaining 1 Tbsp sugar overtop. Cut four or five 1-inch-long slits in the top of the pie.

Bake the pie for 15 minutes, then turn down the temperature to 350°F and bake for another 35–40 minutes, or until the crust is deep golden and the fruit filling is bubbling. Let cool slightly and serve with vanilla ice cream or sharp cheddar cheese.

This will keep, loosely wrapped, in the fridge for up to 1 week.

forest

Wild Plum Clafoutis

SERVES 8-10

10–15 wild plums or prune
  plums
2 eggs
⅔ cup granulated sugar
1 tsp fine sea salt
2 Tbsp melted butter, plus
  more for buttering the
  dish
¾ cup all-purpose flour
1 tsp baking powder
1 tsp ground cardamom
½ tsp ground nutmeg
½ cup milk, divided
2 Tbsp lemon juice

Harvest and its bounty have a special place in my heart. Seeing tables over-flowing with produce at markets— the reward for hours of weeding and long evenings in the garden—makes my heart overflow. For some reason, wild plums signal the beginning of that season for me. Maybe it's because the first tree I could climb was our little plum tree, or maybe I just love how sweet they are and how easily they pull away from the pit. Whatever the reason, this simple plum cake represents to me bounty and harvest and the end of summer. Serve this on a still warm evening and enjoy every bite. —EL

Preheat the oven to 400°F. Place the rack in the centre position of the oven. Generously butter an 11- × 7-inch baking pan or a 9-inch springform pan.

Wash the plums, slice in half, and discard the pits. Arrange the plums in a single layer (some overlapping is okay) to cover the bottom of the prepared pan. Set aside.

In a mixing bowl, whisk the eggs, sugar, and salt together until fully combined, then add the melted butter.

In a small bowl, sift in the flour and baking powder and spices. Add half the flour to the egg mixture, folding to combine, then mix in half the milk. Repeat with the remaining flour and milk, and then add the lemon juice. Mix until you have a loose, glossy batter.

Pour the batter over the plums and tap the dish gently to remove any air bubbles.

Bake for 30–35 minutes, until a toothpick inserted in the centre comes out clean and the batter is golden and puffed. Remove from the oven and run a knife around the outside. It will deflate, so don't panic. Let sit for at least 10 minutes before removing the edges of the pan, if using a springform pan, and cutting.

This will keep in an airtight container in the fridge for up to 1 week.

Forest Berry Crisp
with Lemon Thyme Ice Cream

SERVES 6

Ice cream
6 egg yolks
1 cup granulated sugar
¼ cup lemon juice
1½ cups whole milk
¾ cup whipping (35%)
    cream
4 sprigs of thyme, plus
    extra thyme for garnish
Grated zest of 2 lemons,
    about 1 tsp, mixed with
    a little sugar, for garnish

Filling
⅔ cup granulated sugar
¼ cup cornstarch
½ tsp fine sea salt
½ tsp ground nutmeg
2 cups fresh blackberries
1 cup fresh raspberries
1 cup fresh blueberries
2 Tbsp lemon juice

Topping
1½ cups all-purpose flour
2 tsp baking powder
1 tsp ground cinnamon
¾ cup packed brown sugar
½ cup melted unsalted
    butter

Being able to forage in the forest for berries is just one of the food-related benefits of living here on Vancouver Island. And after a day's foraging, baking them up in this dish makes for a delicious end to a wonderful day in the woods. (Note: Frozen berries work just as well as fresh here. Simply increase the cornstarch by 2 Tbsp and the cooking time by 10 minutes.) —EL

Prepare your ice cream maker as per the manufacturer's instructions.

In a mixing bowl, whisk together the yolks, sugar, and lemon juice until frothy.

In a saucepan over medium heat, bring the milk, cream, thyme, and zest just to a simmer.

Ladle 1 cup of the warm milk mixture into the yolk mixture, whisking to temper the yolks. Pour the yolks into the remaining milk mixture and simmer until it is thick enough to coat the back of a spoon. Remove from the heat and strain through a fine-mesh sieve into a bowl, discarding any solids.

Cover the bowl with plastic wrap, making sure it touches the surface of the mixture, and refrigerate until cold.

Pour the cold ice cream base into the ice cream maker. Follow the manufacturer's instructions to churn the ice cream. Transfer to a 9- × 5-inch loaf pan. Garnish with a few thyme leaves and the sugared lemon zest. Cover and freeze for 6–8 hours, until fully frozen.

Preheat the oven to 350°F.

To make the filling, in a mixing bowl, whisk together the sugar, cornstarch, salt, and nutmeg. Add all the berries, followed by the lemon juice, and toss to coat. Transfer to a 13- × 9-inch baking dish.

To make the topping, in the same bowl, mix together the flour, baking powder, and cinnamon. Mix in the sugar and butter to form a crumbly mixture. Spread evenly over the berries.

Place the dish on a rimmed baking sheet and bake for 35–40 minutes, until the top is golden and the berries are bubbling. Let stand for 10 minutes before serving with ice cream on top.

The fruit crisp will keep in an airtight container in the fridge for up to 1 week. The ice cream will keep, covered, in the freezer for up to 3 months.

No-Bake Chèvre and Salal Berry Cheesecake

SERVES 4

Sauce
½ cup water
1 Tbsp lemon juice
2 Tbsp granulated sugar
2 tsp cornstarch
1 cup salal berries

Cheesecake
2 cups chèvre, at room
    temperature
¼ cup granulated sugar
2 Tbsp lemon juice
2 cups whipping (35%)
    cream, chilled
1 tsp pure vanilla extract
8 graham crackers
4 mason jars
4 rosemary sprigs

Not just great with game meats, salal berries really shine as a perfect balance to the smooth, sweet tang of chèvre. If you can't forage for salal berries, you can substitute the same volume of organic blueberries from your local farmers market. The two are pretty much interchangeable, although salal berries have an earthier, almost herby note that blueberries lack. —DLA

To make the sauce, place the water, lemon juice, sugar, and cornstarch in a small saucepan and stir to combine. Cook over medium heat. As soon as the sauce starts to thicken, add the salal berries. Turn down the heat to low and cook just until the berries begin to break down. Remove from the heat and let cool.

In a stand mixer fitted with paddle attachment, beat the chèvre with the sugar and lemon juice on medium-high speed for 3 minutes, until fluffy and smooth, scraping down the sides of the bowl as needed. Set aside.

Using the stand mixer and paddle attachment again, beat the cream with the vanilla on high speed until stiff peaks form, 5–6 minutes.

Using a spatula, fold the chèvre loosely into the whipped cream. You don't need to completely combine the two; just swirl them together.

To assemble, crumble two graham crackers per person into a small mason jar and top with about 1 cup of the chèvre and whipped cream mixture. Top with 3-4 tablespoons of berry mixture and garnish with a sprig of rosemary.

forest

Backyard Fresh Fig and Thyme Galette

with Salted Caramel Drizzle

Galette

½ cup full-fat sour cream

2 eggs, divided

4 Tbsp honey, divided

1 tsp pure vanilla extract

1 batch of chilled galette
  pastry (page 74)

4 sprigs thyme, leaves only,
  divided, plus additional
  thyme leaves and sprigs
  for garnish

1 lb fresh figs, halved

Coarse sugar

Caramel

¾ cup granulated sugar

1 Tbsp water

⅓ cup whipping (35%)
  cream

1 tsp flaked sea salt

I live for fig season. This simple galette is the perfect way to showcase fresh figs at their peak of ripeness. The thyme adds a wonderful savoury quality that beautifully balances the sweetness. —EL

Preheat the oven to 375°F. Line a baking tray with parchment paper.

In a small bowl, whisk together the sour cream, 1 egg, 2 Tbsp honey, and vanilla. It will be quite runny.

Roll the pastry dough into a 12-inch circle on a well-floured surface. Transfer to the prepared baking sheet. Slowly pour the sour cream mixture into the centre of the dough, using the back of a spoon to spread it into a 9-inch circle. Sprinkle with half the thyme leaves. Arrange the figs, cut side up on the sour cream, drizzle with the remaining 2 Tbsp honey, sprinkle with the reserved thyme. Fold up the edges of the pastry, overlapping them slightly. Whisk the remaining egg and brush it on the pastry. Sprinkle with coarse sugar.

Bake for 45–50 minutes, until the pastry is golden and the figs are juicy. Let sit for 15 minutes before serving warm or let rest, uncovered, for 2–3 hours.

When ready to serve, make the caramel. Place the sugar in a medium saucepan with the water. Bring to a boil over medium-high heat. When the sugar has darkened to a deep caramel, remove from the heat. Stir in the cream. It will bubble up, but keeping stirring until it is fully incorporated. Drizzle this generously over the galette and sprinkle with flaked sea salt. Garnish with extra thyme leaves and sprigs, if desired. Serve immediately.

This will keep, loosely covered, in the fridge for up to 1 week.

forest

Blackberry and Cream Ice Pops

MAKES 10 ICE POPS

2 cups blackberries

2 Tbsp lemon juice

¾ cup granulated sugar, divided

½ cup whipping (35%) cream

1 cup plain Greek-style yogurt

1 tsp pure vanilla extract

Summer isn't quite summer unless ice pops are involved, and on the West Coast, they had better contain roadside blackberries. Blackberries are so prolific here that they really are in every sense a weed. They grow on fences and in ditches and will invade any garden that catches their eye. Luckily, they are also incredibly loved. It is common to walk into a bakery and see a sign by the cash register saying "$5 per bucket of blackberries." Kids will spend their August days picking berries to make a few extra bucks. And at the end of one of those days, nothing is better to come home to than one of these pops. —EL

Wash and shake dry the berries. Place them in a small bowl, drizzle with the lemon juice, sprinkle with ¼ cup of the sugar, and stir to combine. Refrigerate for 1 hour to set, then mash the berries gently and refrigerate again until ready to use.

In a small saucepan over medium heat, place the remaining ½ cup of sugar and the cream. Whisk to combine then simmer, without whisking, until the sugar dissolves. Remove from the heat and whisk in the yogurt and vanilla. Refrigerate, covered, for 2–3 hours, until completely chilled.

Place 1 Tbsp of yogurt mixture in the bottom of each ice pop mold, then, alternating between berries and yogurt, fill them to within ¼–½ inch of the top. Add the sticks or tops of the molds and place in the freezer to freeze completely, 6 hours or up to overnight.

To unmold, place in warm water for 10–15 seconds to gently loosen, then remove the pops. Return to the freezer on a parchment lined-baking sheet to refreeze for up to 3 months or serve immediately.

Lilac Celebration Cake

Lilac simple syrup
1 cup granulated sugar
1¼ cups water
1 cup lilac blossoms

Cake
10 eggs
¾ cup granulated sugar
2¼ cups all-purpose flour
1 tsp baking powder

Buttercream
2¼ cups unsalted butter,
    room temperature
10 cups sifted icing sugar
½ cup satsuma orange
    juice (from about
    2 satsumas)
2 Tbsp lilac simple syrup

Lilac blossoms for garnish

I wish lilacs had a longer season—their blooms and intoxicating scent never fail to lift my spirits. When I realized lilacs were edible and tasted exactly like the way they smell, I started scouring the neighbourhood at all hours of the night. The lilac simple syrup in this recipe is also delicious in tea or coffee, cocktails, cookies, and frostings. In the warm parts of the Cowichan Valley and Saanich Peninsula nurseries grow citrus fruits, but they won't be available at the same time lilac blossoms are, so just go with citrus from the market. —EL

To make the simple syrup, in a saucepan over medium heat, add the sugar to the water. Stir gently to combine, bring to a simmer to dissolve the sugar, and remove from the heat. Add the lilac blossoms and submerge, stirring gently to coat. Let cool to room temperature, stirring every few minutes to ensure the flavour is seeping into the syrup. Taste after 15 minutes. It should taste intensely of lilac. The blossoms can stay in the syrup for up to 12 hours. Strain the syrup, discarding the blossoms, and store in an airtight container in the fridge until needed, or for up to 3 weeks.

Preheat the oven to 350°F. Grease four 8-inch round cake pans with butter.

To make the cake, in the bowl of a stand mixer fitted with the whisk attachment, whisk the eggs on medium speed for 3 minutes, until a creamy pale colour. Stop the mixer and sprinkle the sugar evenly over the eggs. Begin on the lowest speed and gradually increase the speed to high. Whisk for 10 minutes, until the egg mixture has tripled in volume.

In a bowl, whisk together the flour and baking powder.

Remove the bowl from the stand mixer. Sprinkle 2–3 Tbsp of the flour mixture over the surface of the egg mixture and gently fold it in. Repeat with the remaining flour. The batter is ready when it is streak-free with no traces of flour showing.

Divide the batter evenly between the four prepared cake pans, smoothing the tops. The batter will be shallow. Bake in the centre of the oven for 25 minutes, until a toothpick inserted into the centre of a cake comes out with only a few crumbs attached. Immediately, run a knife around each pan to loosen. Invert the cakes onto a wire rack. Using a toothpick, poke the cakes deeply (but not all the way through, or the syrup will pour out the bottom!) all over their surfaces. Drizzle ¼ cup of syrup evenly over each cake, spreading it with a pastry brush. Let the cakes cool completely.

To make the buttercream, beat the butter using a stand or hand-held mixer, until light and fluffy. Slowly begin adding the icing sugar, allowing it to incorporate before adding more, scraping down the bowl as required. Gently mix in the satsuma juice, then add the syrup. Beat for 2–3 minutes to fully combine.

(Continued on page 207)

(Continued from page 204)

To assemble the cake, spread ¼ of the buttercream evenly over the first layer of cake, using an offset spatula. Repeat with the remaining layers. Before icing the top, place a small amount of the remaining buttercream on the offset spatula and run a thin, even layer of buttercream around the outside of the cake, allowing the layers to still be visible and smoothing any buttercream that oozes out between the layers. Spread the remaining buttercream on the top of the cake and smooth.

Serve topped with fresh lilac blossoms.

This will keep in an airtight container in the fridge for up to 3 days.

forest

Spiced Rosehip and Crabapple Jelly

MAKES 6 JARS

2 lb rosehips

2 lb crabapples, cored, quartered

1 cinnamon stick

1 Tbsp whole cloves

2 tsp whole black peppercorns

Granulated sugar

Lemon juice

2 Tbsp unsalted butter

Rosehips are those glorious red seed pods that appear on wild rose bushes around the end of summer. They're delightful to gather and delicious when turned into jelly or syrup. They also pack a vitamin C punch, perfect for the dark winter months. I like to serve this with my ferryman's platter (page 118). —DLA

Place the rosehips in a large saucepan, cover with 3 inches of water, and bring to a boil over high heat. Turn down the heat and simmer, uncovered, for 40 minutes.

Add the crabapples to the pan with the cinnamon stick, cloves, peppercorns, and enough water to cover all the fruit. Return to a boil, turn down the heat, cover, and simmer for 15 minutes, or until the fruit is very soft.

Remove the pan from the heat and pour the fruit and juices into a jelly bag placed over a large, clean saucepan. Leave overnight to let the juices drip through.

In the morning, place a couple of dessert plates in the freezer. Measure the juice in the saucepan: For each 1 cup of juice, add 1 cup of sugar, and 1 tsp of lemon juice. Bring to a boil over medium heat, stirring to dissolve the sugar. Boil hard for 5–15 minutes until the setting point is reached. Test for this by pouring 1 tsp of the liquid onto a frozen plate. Let it set for a few seconds and then push it with your finger. It will wrinkle up when it's reached the jelly point.

Remove the jelly from the heat and stir in the butter to remove the foam. Pour into sterilized jars, seal, and process in a water bath, following standard canning jar instructions. Store in a cool, dark place for up to 1 year.

forest

Bannock and Easy Blackberry Freezer Jam

SERVES 6–8

Jam
3 cups fresh blackberries
1 cup granulated sugar
2 tsp lemon juice

Bannock
3 cups all-purpose flour
2 Tbsp baking powder
1 tsp fine sea salt
¼ cup butter, melted
1½ cups water
3 Tbsp vegetable oil

Originally brought to North America by early Scottish explorers, bannock quickly became a regular dish for Canada's First Nations. These are great slathered in butter and blackberry freezer jam, or, alternatively, try them alongside a hearty stew instead of bread. —DLA

To make the jam, place all the ingredients in a medium saucepan over medium heat. Let cook, stirring occasionally, until the berries begin to break apart and the sugar dissolves. Crush the berries with the back of a wooden spoon and continue to heat until the mixture comes together in a jammy consistency, about 15 minutes. Remove from the heat and let cool in the pan. Transfer to clean mason jars and refrigerate for up to 1 week or freeze for up to 6 months.

To make the bannocks, place the flour, baking powder, and salt in a large bowl. Stir to combine. Pour in the melted butter, followed by the water. Stir with a fork until everything is incorporated.

Turn the dough out onto a lightly floured work surface and, using your hands, knead gently until the mixture comes together into a ball. Divide the ball in half and press each one into a disc about ½-inch thick.

Heat the oil in a 9-inch cast iron skillet over medium heat and add the dough. Bake for 10 minutes per side, or until deeply golden and a toothpick inserted into the centre comes out clean. Serve warm with butter and jam. You can store these in an airtight container in the fridge for up to 5 days.

forest

Lilac Vodka Soda

2 Tbsp lilac simple syrup
  (page 204)
2 oz vodka
2 dashes lime juice
4 oz soda water
Ice cubes
Lilac blossoms, for garnish

The day that I realized lilacs were edible was a really great day. Their scent is one of my favourites, so when I discovered that they taste the way they smell and that their scent and flavour can be captured in a simple syrup, life became forever better. The colour of the syrup is just beautiful, especially if you find some deeply coloured purple blossoms, making this cocktail look as good as it tastes. —EL

Divide the simple syrup, vodka, and lime juice evenly between two cocktail glasses. Swirl or stir with a bar spoon to combine. Top with soda water and add enough ice cubes to fill the glass to the rim. Garnish with blossoms and serve immediately.

Tayberry and Basil Mojito

Simple Syrup
1 cup water
1 cup granulated sugar
8–10 large basil leaves, plus
   more for garnish

Cocktail
½ cup tayberries, plus
   more berries for garnish
Ice cubes
4 oz white rum
2 oz soda water

Tasty and refreshing in the peak of summer, tayberries are tart like raspberries, juicy like blackberries, and a lovely burgundy colour. They match the savoury-sweet basil to create a tasty cocktail that will create memories for summers to come. Many visitors to Vancouver Island don't realize that we have very hot, dry summers, perfect for growing basil in pots, and our mild winter days lets us seamlessly transfer the basil to our kitchen windowsills. Herbs grow prolifically here: My neighbour's front lawn is oregano and thyme! (Note: If you can't get tayberries, use ¼ cup blackberries and ¼ cup raspberries.) —EL

In a saucepan over medium heat, bring the water and sugar to just a boil, stirring to melt the sugar. Remove from the heat and pour the warm syrup into a clean mason jar. Add the basil leaves, put the lid on the jar, and refrigerate to allow the basil to steep for at least 3 hours, or up to overnight.

When you're ready to make the cocktail, place the tayberries and 2 Tbsp of the basil simple syrup in a cocktail shaker and muddle. Add a handful of ice cubes and the rum and shake vigorously to blend.

Place two large ice cubes in two Tom Collins glasses. Strain in the mojito, dividing it evenly between the two glasses. Top each glass with soda and garnish with extra tayberries and basil leaves. Enjoy immediately.

The simple syrup will keep in the fridge for 1 week with the basil leaves sitting in the syrup. Remove the leaves after 1 week and the syrup will last for 3 months in the fridge.

Golden Spiced Vodka

MAKES 8 CUPS

3 (each 750 mL) bottles
   good-quality vodka
2 cups granulated sugar
2 lb golden plums
¼ cup whole cloves
5–6 star anise
3 cinnamon sticks

I make a large batch of this every year when our plum tree becomes heavy with ripe, juicy fruit. It takes a bit of patience and attention, but I promise that the results are well worth the effort. Come the holiday season, you'll have a delicious, golden elixir that tastes like Christmas in a glass. I like to serve it straight, but for a nice cocktail you can add some sparkling soda and garnish with a cinnamon stick. —DLA

Thoroughly clean a 1 gallon glass container and pour in the vodka and sugar. Mix to combine. Wash the plums well and then, using a fork or sharp skewer, poke holes into each one and place them in the jar. Cut a piece of parchment paper large enough to cover the surface of the plums and place it over them, pushing down on the fruit to submerge them and have some of the vodka sitting overtop the paper. Seal the jar and place it in a cool, dark spot. Shake the jar every few days to stir the fruit juice and vodka together. This is a slow process, but well worth the wait.

After 8 weeks, remove the parchment and add the cloves and star anise. Give the mixture a stir and replace the parchment with a new piece. Tuck the jar away from the light again. Give it a shake every day for the next 10 days, then add the cinnamon sticks and repeat for another 10 days.

Strain the vodka from all the solids and transfer the liquid to sterilized glass bottles. Serve straight-up as cold as possible.

This will keep in the freezer for up to 1 year.

Easy Elderflower Champagne

MAKES 8 QUARTS

8 quarts water

2.2 lb granulated sugar

10 elderflower heads,
   cleaned, stalks removed

5 lemons, halved and
   juiced

1 vanilla bean, split open
   lengthwise, seeds intact

Champagne yeast,
   if needed

Elderflower isn't a common ingredient here in Canada, but the trees do grow locally on Vancouver Island, and I am completely in love with their glorious, heady scent. Even if you're not into brewing, this is an easy recipe to follow. (Note: For an alcohol-free version, omit the champagne yeast, remove the flower heads after 48 hours, and boil to reduce by half to form an elderflower concentrate. Bottle immediately and store as below.) —DLA

Place the water, sugar, lemons, lemon juice, and vanilla bean in a large stockpot. Bring to a boil, stirring to dissolve the sugar, and then remove from the heat.

Let the water cool completely. This is crucial, as heat changes the taste of elderflower considerably. Add the flower heads once the water has cooled. Gently stir to incorporate, making sure the flowers are fully submerged. Cover the pot with a clean piece of muslin or towel, secure with string, and leave to ferment in a dark, cool space.

Stir with a wooden spoon every 12 hours to encourage activity. After 24 hours, check for signs of fermentation. The mixture should be starting to bubble and foam. If nothing has happened after 24 hours, add a small pinch of champagne yeast. After 48 hours, remove the flower heads with tongs.

Allow the mixture to ferment for 4 or 5 days then pass it through a fine-mesh sieve and decant into sturdy, sterilized screw-top glass bottles. As the fermentation continues, release excess pressure in the bottles by opening the screw top enough to allow the pressure to release and "burp" the excess gas away.

After 1 week in the bottles, you should have your champagne. Store in the fridge to slow the fermentation. Serve cold. Champagne will keep in the fridge for up to 3 months.

forest

sea

Whenever I'm away from the Island, here's what I miss the most: sitting by the seashore on a driftwood log, listening to the soft lapping of the water as it rhythmically rolls up and falls back, ending with a faint tinkle as the water runs down through the rocks. Nothing compares to the soothing, meditative sound of the water and the freshness of the ocean breeze and salty air. No matter where you are on Vancouver Island, you're never far from the sea. Watch the kelp bob in the waves; pick up a rock and watch the crabs scurry; catch a glimpse of a barnacle with its tentacles out, a fish swimming past, a little crab tottering across the rocks, or an anemone waving in the water. Here you'll see plenty of evidence that our ocean is alive.

The waters on the east side of the Island are quite sheltered by the small islands scattered along the Strait of Georgia, making this the perfect area for prawns, rock and Dungeness crabs, clams, mussels, and, of course, the famed Fanny Bay oysters and the small, sweet Kusshi oysters. On the windswept west side of the Island, protection is relatively nonexistent in most respects as the vast, strong Pacific Ocean stretches out to the horizon as far as the eye can see. This is the domain of salmon, halibut, and cod—the big ocean fish that embrace the open water.

Of all the fish that live in the waters of the Pacific, salmon compel me most because of the story of their life cycles. From mid-October through November, you can visit many rivers—the stream that goes through Goldstream Provincial Park is my favourite—teeming with salmon, all swimming upstream to find the spot where they were born so they can spawn. Remarkably, the salmon are able to locate by scent the spot where they were born, with an accuracy that brings them within a mere few inches. There they lay their eggs, then die shortly after. As sad as this sounds, the flesh provides food and nutrients to their young and also adds many nutrients to the soil. When the eggs start hatching, the river once again overflows, this time with little fish making their way to the ocean to live their lives. If you head down to a river to see the little fish hatching, be forewarned that it's really smelly; you may also catch a glimpse of nearby wildlife as they feast.

While the salmon are spawning, you may also witness fishers practicing traditional fishing techniques that are indigenous to the area. There are, in fact, many different traditional methods of fishing during spawning season, perhaps with a spear or net attached to a very long pole. Islanders care about the salmon population, and it is common to see researchers in the water counting fish during spawning season as they work hard to ensure that our fishing practices and ocean stay healthy and sustainable.

At the north end of the Island you can find the widest variety of fish, especially through the northern passage and down through Desolation Sound. Here, the salmon, halibut, and cod are plentiful, as are red snapper and many species of rockfish, ling cod, and even albacore tuna. The mix of the cold open ocean and surrounding sheltered islands and inlets creates the perfect ecosystem in which the fish can live.

Our oceans are special. They are alive and need to be cared for. Islanders are reminded of this every day as we see the ocean, travel over it, and experience it in all its forms—from the winter gales that toss huge logs onto the coastal roads, to the warm, summer tidepools and aquamarine water that is reminiscent of the tropics. We are blessed to experience it and cannot take it for granted.

The recipes that follow all feature the bounty of our sea. Indulge in sweet spot prawns and summer beach crab boils; shuck oysters on the docks, and savour delicious poached halibut and grilled salmon. Each flavor is unique, delicious, and as local as it can be. My hope is that you not only get a taste of our ocean but also treasure all that it offers. —EL

sea

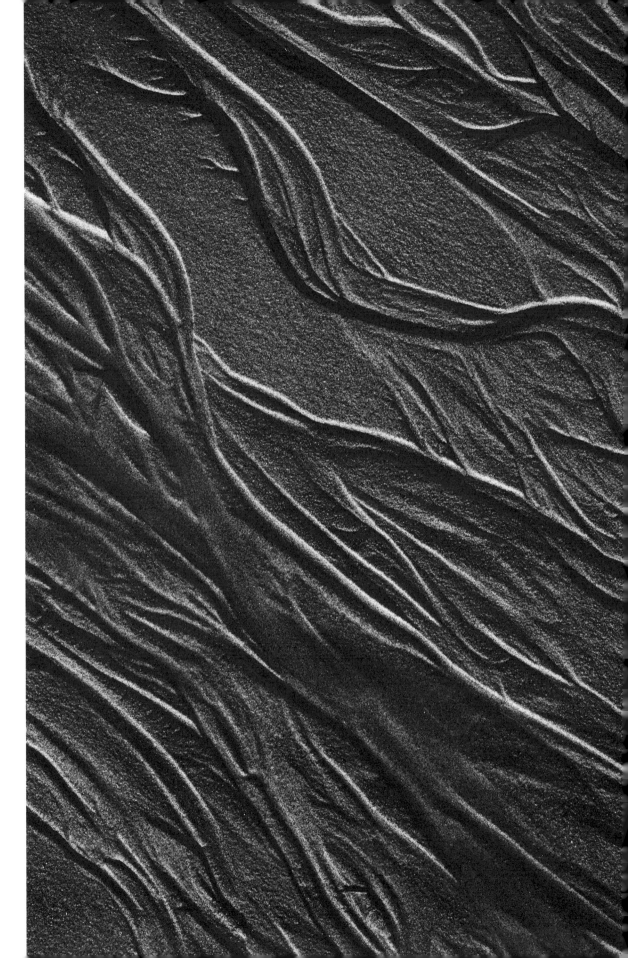

sea

Crab Cake Breakfast Benny

with Dill Seed Hollandaise

SERVES 4

Crab cakes

1 medium cooking onion, diced

⅓ cup vegetable oil, divided

1½ lb Dungeness crabmeat, well drained, all shells removed

2 Tbsp finely chopped fresh chives

2 tsp grated lemon zest

2 tsp lemon juice

2 tsp smoked paprika

1 tsp fine sea salt

1 tsp cracked black pepper

5 large eggs, divided

1¾ cups panko bread crumbs, divided

1 Tbsp water

Hollandaise sauce

5 egg yolks

2½ Tbsp lemon juice

1 cup unsalted butter, melted

2 tsp ground dill seed

Flaked sea salt

Cracked black pepper

Eggs and Assembly

2 Tbsp white wine vinegar

8 eggs

2 ripe avocados, thinly sliced

Fine sea salt and cracked black pepper

Eggs Benedict is officially my favourite dish on the planet, and I am always trying to find new and interesting variations. Rather than topping an English muffin or bagel with crabmeat, I thought to myself, why not make a crispy crab cake the base itself? The results were so good that this is now the number one request from my seafood-loving friends, especially when made with freshly caught, local Dungeness crabs from our traps. —DLA

Preheat the oven to 220°F. Line a baking sheet with parchment paper.

To make the crab cakes, in a skillet over medium-high heat, place the onion and 2 Tbsp of the oil. Sauté, stirring once or twice, until the onions begin to caramelize, about 5 minutes. Do not let them begin to burn. Turn down the heat and continue to sauté until the onions are a deep golden colour. Remove from the heat, transfer to a mixing bowl, and let cool slightly.

Add the crabmeat, chives, lemon zest and juice, paprika, salt, and pepper to the onions. Lightly beat 3 of the eggs and add them to the crab mixture, along with ¾ cup of the panko. Mix everything together and, using your hands, form eight evenly sized patties. Place on the prepared sheet and pop them in the freezer, uncovered, for at least 30 minutes, and up to 1 hour.

Prepare a dredging station: Beat the 2 remaining eggs with the water in a shallow dish. Place the remaining 1 cup of panko in another shallow dish. Dip each crab cake first into the egg mixture, coating fully and evenly and shaking off any excess, and then into the panko, coating fully and evenly and shaking off any excess.

Heat the remaining oil in a large skillet over medium-low heat. Cook the crab cakes for 4 minutes per side, or until crispy and golden brown. You may have to do this in batches. Keep the cooked crab cakes warm in the oven, on a baking sheet, until you're ready to eat.

To make the hollandaise sauce, in the top half of a double-boiler (or a small stainless steel bowl), whisk the egg yolks and lemon juice together until the mixture begins to thicken slightly. Place the egg yolk and lemon juice mixture on top of the double boiler base set to a simmer (or if using a metal bowl, place on top of a small saucepan containing an inch or two of simmering water). Whisking constantly, slowly drizzle in the melted butter. The sauce should thicken again quite quickly. Remove from the heat and whisk in the dill seed and a pinch of salt and pepper. Cover until ready to use. If the sauce is too thick when you come to use it, stir in 1 Tbsp of hot water to get a pouring consistency.

To prepare the eggs, fill a medium-sized saucepan with 3–4 inches of water and add the vinegar. Bring the water to a low boil, then turn down the temperature to bring it to a simmer. Crack the eggs one at a time into a small bowl (to ensure the yolks do not break) and carefully slide each egg into the water. You may have to do this in batches. Bring the water temperature back up slightly to maintain a low boil. Using a large slotted spoon, very carefully lift each egg off the bottom of the saucepan so it doesn't stick. Cook the eggs for about 4 minutes for a soft-medium poach, or to your preferred doneness—but remember that they will continue to cook after they have been removed from the heat.

Remove the crab cakes from the oven and top each with avocado. Using a slotted spoon, remove the eggs from the water and place one on each avocado-topped crab cake. Garnish each with about ½ cup of warm Hollandaise sauce and season to taste with salt and pepper. Serve immediately.

Corn and Cod Fritters
with Roasted Tomato Mayo

MAKES 24 FRITTERS

Roasted tomato mayo
3 Roma tomatoes, cut in
  half lengthwise
2 Tbsp olive oil
1 cup full-fat mayonnaise
Flake sea salt and ground
  black pepper

Fritters
Vegetable oil, for deep
  frying
½ lb ling cod or other rock
  fish, cut into ½-inch
  pieces
1 cup chickpea flour
½ medium cooking onion,
  finely diced
1 cup frozen (thawed) or
  fresh corn kernels
½ cup chopped cilantro
  leaves
1 Tbsp crushed red pepper
  flakes
½ tsp baking powder
½ tsp fine sea salt
1 cup lukewarm water

I learned the method for these fritters from Debbie, an Indian woman I used to work with who would make the best pakoras for staff lunches. I took what I learned from her and added my own twist by using local ingredients and one of my favourite food combinations. —DLA

Preheat the oven to 385°F. Line a rimmed baking sheet with parchment paper.

To make the mayo, cut the tomatoes in half and place them cut side down on the prepared baking sheet. Drizzle them with the oil and roast for 20–25 minutes, or until soft and wrinkly. Remove from the oven and let cool on the pan. Pulse the cooled tomatoes with the mayo in a food processor until well incorporated. Add a pinch of salt and pepper and set aside, covered, at room temperature.

To make the fritters, fill a large skillet or cast-iron Dutch oven with 1½–2 inches of vegetable oil. Heat the oil to 370°F (a candy thermometer is ideal for this).

In a large bowl, stir together the cod, flour, onion, corn, cilantro, red pepper flakes, baking powder, and salt. Mixing vigorously with a wooden spoon, slowly add the water until the batter has the texture of Greek yogurt and is slightly bubbly throughout. You may not need all of the water.

Using two spoons and working in small batches, carefully place heaping tablespoonfuls of batter in the hot oil. Turn them when the undersides are a deep golden brown, 2–3 minutes per side. Drain on paper towels. Serve immediately with the mayo.

The mayo will keep in an airtight container in the fridge for up to 1 week but the fritters are best eaten the same day they're made.

Individual Smoked Salmon Terrines

SERVES 6

1½ cups full-fat cream
    cheese, room
    temperature, cubed

⅓ cup lemon juice

¼ cup whipping (35%)
    cream

½ cup chopped fresh dill

2 Tbsp chopped fresh
    chives

1 Tbsp finely minced
    shallot

2 tsp fresh cracked green
    peppercorns

1 cup flaked hot-smoked
    salmon

2 Tbsp capers

6 slices lox

Terrines come in all shapes and sizes, although most often a loaf tin is the best receptacle to make them in. Most pork and chicken terrines are cooked, but this recipe uses smoked salmon, so it's easy to toss together and put in the fridge. Here I decided to make individual terrines, so you don't have to worry about double-dipping at a party. I keep mine in the fridge or freezer in a muffin tin and pop them out as needed. —EL

In a stand mixer fitted with the whisk attachment, beat the cream cheese until lump-free. Add the lemon juice and cream and continue to beat until fully combined. Scrape down the bowl and add the herbs, shallot, and peppercorns. Starting on slow speed and gradually working up to medium-high, beat for 1 minute. Scrape down the bowl and beat on medium-high for 1 minute more. Scrape down the bowl and add the flaked salmon. Beat on low until fully combined. Fold in the capers. Cover and refrigerate, 30 minutes to overnight.

Line the cups of a standard muffin tin with a square of plastic wrap, letting the plastic hang over the cups. Place some lox in each cup.

Remove the terrine from the fridge and fill the cups of the muffin tin with it, tapping the pan to remove any air bubbles. Cover with plastic wrap and place in the freezer for at least 2–3 hours. Remove from the freezer 1–2 hours before you plan to eat and put it in the fridge to soften.

To serve the terrines, pull off the top layer of plastic wrap to remove them from the muffin tin. Enjoy immediately.

The terrines will keep up to 3 months in the freezer. Once thawed they will keep in the fridge in an airtight container for up to 3 days. Do not refreeze them.

sea

Gin-Cured Salmon

MAKES 1 SIDE –
24 SERVINGS

6 Tbsp coarse sea salt

2 Tbsp granulated sugar

2 Tbsp finely chopped dill

1 tsp grated lemon zest

2 dried juniper berries, ground

3 Tbsp good-quality gin

3 lb side coho or wild sockeye salmon

Don't be daunted by the idea of curing salmon yourself as it's actually much easier than you might imagine. The sugar, salt, and alcohol combine to do their magic and then it's just a matter of time. I love this with a bagel and cream cheese or served alongside some Quick Summer Farm Pickles (page 44). The Victoria Distillers' Empress Gin adds a nice touch of colour as well as a heady juniper note. —DLA

Combine the salt, sugar, dill, lemon zest, juniper berries, and gin in a small bowl. This is your cure.

Place the salmon on a piece of parchment paper large enough to cover it completely. Rub the entire piece of fish, on both sides, with the salt mixture. Fold the parchment over the salmon and wrap it tightly in plastic wrap. Place the wrapped fish in the fridge, sandwiched between two baking sheets and weighed down with a cast iron pan or some cans of food. Leave it like this for 48 hours.

Take the salmon out of the fridge and remove the plastic and parchment paper. Pour off any liquid and wipe off the excess cure. Do not rinse the fish. Using a very sharp knife, cut the salmon into very thin slices across the grain. Use immediately or refrigerate until ready to serve.

sea

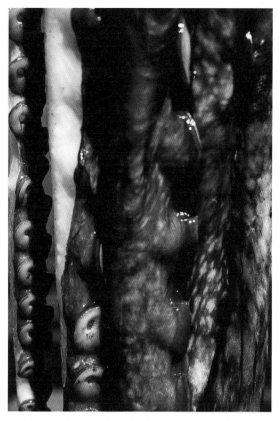

sea

Apple Cider and Cream-Braised Qualicum Bay Clams

SERVES 4

1 pint hard cider
½ cup whipping (35%)
  cream
4 sprigs thyme
½-inch piece of ginger,
  peeled
2 lb fresh clams

Sweet and delicious and so simple you barely need a recipe, these braised clams are always a winner. If Qualicum Bay clams are not available, use any fresh clams from a seafood market. Just make sure the shells aren't cracked and none of the clams are open. If I'm feeling adventurous, I'll use local Sea Cider Farm & Ciderhouse's seasonal Ginger Perry cider for a soft yet spicy version of this recipe. —EL

In a large saucepan over medium-high heat, bring the cider and cream just to a boil. Turn down the heat to medium so it simmers gently. Add the thyme and ginger and continue to simmer for 2–3 minutes so they infuse fully into the cider-cream mixture.

Wash the clams (see page 246). Discard any that have opened.

Increase the heat to medium and add the clams to the pan. Cover and simmer for 4–5 minutes, just until the clams have opened. Remove from the heat and, using a slotted spoon, transfer the clams to a serving bowl. Discard any that did not open. Spoon a few ladlefuls of sauce over the clams and serve immediately.

Clams should be eaten as soon as they are cooked. The sauce will keep in an airtight container in the fridge for up to 1 week.

sea

Creamy Crab, Caraway Jill, and Black Kale Dip

SERVES 4

4 large black Tuscan kale
   leaves
4 Tbsp extra virgin olive
   oil, divided
2 garlic cloves, minced
1 shallot, minced
2 Tbsp all-purpose flour
½ cup full-fat cream
   cheese, cubed
1 cup milk
1 cup grated Caraway Jill
   cheese, plus more grated
   cheese for the topping
1 cup flaked crabmeat
Coarse sea salt and ground
   black pepper

Not quite crab dip, not quite spinach dip, this warm cheese-filled, super-flavourful dip is a simple summer barbecue appetizer. Of course, fresh crab—especially Dungeness or rock —is the very best for this, but canned is easily substituted. Caraway Jill cheese is one of my favourites from Little Qualicum Cheeseworks, an amazing local cheese company. It is softer and sweeter than Monterey Jack and is dotted with caraway seeds throughout. (Note: You can also use the same volume of Monterey Jack and 2 tsp of caraway seeds.) —EL

Remove the stems from the kale and cut the leaves into ¼-inch-wide ribbons. Place the ribbons in a small bowl and drizzle with 1 Tbsp of oil. Massage the kale well. It will turn a deep emerald colour. Set aside.

In a medium saucepan over medium heat, warm the remaining 3 Tbsp oil and add the garlic and shallot. Sauté for 2 minutes, until translucent, then add the flour. Cook, stirring constantly to remove any lumps, until the flour is creamy coloured. Add all the cream cheese, letting it melt as you stir the roux. When it starts to boil, gradually add the milk, stirring constantly. The sauce will thicken quickly. Just continue to add the milk, stirring, until the mixture is thick and creamy. Turn the heat to low. Mix in the kale to coat, then add the grated cheese and stir for 2–3 minutes, until melted. Remove from the heat. Stir in the crab and season to taste with salt and pepper. Transfer to an ovenproof serving dish.

For an extra-cheesy dip, sprinkle more grated cheese overtop and broil for 1–2 minutes. Serve immediately with crackers or crostini.

This will keep, covered, in the fridge overnight and can be rewarmed before eating, but it really is best the day it is made.

Mussels Steamer Bowl in Ortega Crème

SERVES 4

2 lb fresh mussels

1 red onion, finely
chopped

2 garlic cloves, finely
chopped

2 Tbsp salted butter

1½ cups Ortega or other
dry white wine

½ cup whipping (35%)
cream

¼ cup fennel fronds

4 sprigs thyme

1 bay leaf

¼ tsp cayenne pepper

*To clean mussels or clams, scrub
the shells in cold running water
to remove any dirt or barnacles.
If mussels still have their beards
on, grab a hold of them and pull
toward the pointy tip of the shell
to remove them.*

Classic French-style mussels with an island twist sums up this dish. Salt Spring mussels are big and juicy and packed with flavour. Quickly braising them in an Ortega crème sauce with fresh herbs and butter shows you can actually improve on perfection! Ortega is a German white grape variety commonly grown on Vancouver Island. Many local wineries produce delicious and even award-winning vintages. —EL

Clean the mussels (see below). Discard any that are open or cracked.

In a large saucepan over medium heat, sauté the onion and garlic in the butter until they are just starting to turn golden and the butter is bubbling. Add all the wine and cream and bring to a simmer. Stir in the fennel, thyme, bay leaf, and cayenne. Simmer for 10 minutes to allow the flavours to infuse the broth and for the broth to reduce slightly. Do not let it come to a boil.

Add the mussels, cover, and allow to simmer for another 3–4 minutes, until the shells are fully open. Discard any mussels whose shells did not open. Using a slotted spoon, transfer the mussels to a serving bowl and ladle with some of the broth. Serve with crusty bread or frites for a classic French feel.

Mussels don't keep well, so enjoy these the day they are made.

sea

Oysters on the Half Shell

with Cucumber Rhubarb Mignonette

SERVES 2

½ cup Champagne vinegar

2 Tbsp finely chopped
    fresh rhubarb

2 Tbsp finely diced peeled
    English cucumber

1 Tbsp finely chopped
    shallot

1 Tbsp granulated sugar

Flaked sea salt

1 dozen shucked fresh, live
    Fanny Bay oysters

1 lemon, cut into thin
    wedges

2 Tbsp freshly grated
    horseradish

When I was a small girl, long before Fanny Bay oysters graced the world's top restaurant menus, my dad and I would walk the beaches collecting buckets of them. He planned on eating them whereas I loved the pearls he would occasionally hand to me. As a child I didn't appreciate the oysters' delicate taste, but Dad would slurp them back right there on the beach, seconds after harvesting them: Now as an adult I adore them. Fanny Bays are medium to large in size and delightfully briny—a perfect foil for the sweet tartness of this mignonette. (See page 250 for tips on how to open oysters.)—DLA

Place the vinegar in a 1-cup mason jar and add the rhubarb, cucumber, chopped shallots, sugar, and a pinch of salt. Cover tightly and shake to combine until the sugar fully dissolves. Refrigerate for at least 1 hour, and up to overnight.

When you're ready to serve, place the shucked oysters on a bed of crushed ice and serve with the mignonette, lemon wedges, and horseradish on the side.

sea

BBQ Smoked Boerenkaas-Topped Oysters

SERVES 4

2 lb cedar wood chips

16 fresh oysters

¼ cup salted butter

2 Tbsp sherry vinegar

2 garlic cloves

1 tsp grated ginger

1 tsp Sriracha or your
favourite hot sauce

½ tsp cracked black pepper

¾ cup grated Boerenkaas
cheese

2 tsp chopped curly leaf
parsley, for garnish

I've heard so many people say they love or hate oysters. My guess is the people in the "hate" camp haven't tried smoked oysters. Smoking them tempers their strong flavour and, I think, makes they taste more like a mussel or a clam.

Smoking is easily done even if you don't have a smoker. I fill an extra grill basket with the soaked wood chips and set them beside the oysters. It work just as well as a smoker. I've also used this method very successfully for chicken and ribs. The smoky Gouda-style cheese in this recipe is called Boerenkaas, a traditional Dutch farmhouse cheese, and it melts perfectly over the oysters. I like to buy mine locally, from Natural Pastures Cheese Company. —EL

Soak the woodchips in cold water for at least 1 hour before you plan to start cooking.

Heat a charcoal or gas grill to high, for about 15 minutes, then turn down the heat to low. Drain the woodchips, place them in a grill basket, and put them on one side of the grill. Let the wood to start to smoke, 10–15 minutes.

Meanwhile, shuck the oysters. This is a bit of an art but this is the best way I've found to do it.

1. Wear gloves. Oysters can be very sharp and often have barnacles. Wash and scrub the shells with a stiff bristle brush.

2. Hold the oyster cup side down in your hand, with the pointy part or hinge facing away from you.

3. Carefully insert a knife (oyster knives are best, of course, but a strong paring knife works well too) at the hinge of the shells and twist it to separate them. You'll hear the hinge pop. Run the blade along the length of the shells, keeping the shells level so you don't lose any juice. Pay attention as you do this so you don't cut yourself.

4. Carefully lift the top shell from the bottom one, keeping the bottom one level, and scrape off any meat still attached to the top shell. Discard any bits of shell or sand you see.

Place the shucked oysters, still on the bottom shell, on a rimmed baking sheet that can go on the grill.

In a small saucepan over medium heat, melt the butter and vinegar together. Crush the garlic cloves and then mince them. Mix garlic cloves in to the butter mixture along with the ginger, Sriracha, and pepper. Using a small spoon, spoon a little bit of the garlic butter sauce over each oyster.

The grill temperature should stay between 250°F and 275°F. Place the tray of oysters on the hot grill and smoke for 25–30 minutes, checking that they aren't cooking too quickly. You want them to feel like Jell-O when you press them gently, and they should still be juicy. If the grill is too hot, the butter will evaporate and they will feel tough. If they are overcooked, they will be tough and chewy.

Lift the lid off the grill. A billow of smoke will probably escape, but that's okay. Sprinkle the top of each oyster with the cheese, close the lid, and let the oysters smoke for 5 more minutes, until the cheese is melted and just starting to bubble. Remove from the grill, transfer to serving plates, garnish each oyster with a sprinkle of parsley, and serve immediately.

Oysters do not keep and should be consumed as soon as they are cooked.

Oysters of Vancouver Island

Vancouver Island oysters are served in many of the top oyster bars across the world—and for good reason. Our temperate Pacific waters nurture some of the sweetest, juiciest breeds around. From the deliciously salty Fanny Bay oysters, to the tiny and beautifully creamy Kusshi, the range of sizes and flavours available makes Vancouver Island an oyster lover's paradise. You'll hear the experts speak of cucumber and melon notes, along with salinity levels and brininess, and it's fun to try to detect those flavour intricacies when you're sampling and savouring. See the BC Oyster Guide for a comprehensive guide to these ocean treats and test yourself the next time you get to indulge to see what flavours you can detect. —DLA

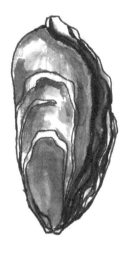

BUCKLEY BAY
Baynes Sound

- extra small to medium
- sweet with low salinity and melon notes

CHEFS CREEK
Chefs Creek of Baynes Sound

- extra small to small
- briny and crisp

FANNY BAY
Baynes Sound

- extra small to medium
- sweet with medium salinity; slightly metallic

KOMO GWAY
Baynes Sound

- extra small to medium
- sweet and briny with cucumber notes

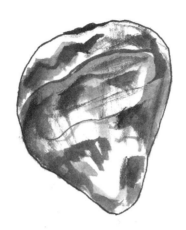

KUSSHI
Baynes Sound

- small
- sweet and meaty with low salinity

MAC'S BEACH
Baynes Sound

- extra small to large
- smooth with low salinity

PHANTOM CREEK
Baynes Sound

- extra small to small
- subtle and slightly briny

SHIP POINT
Baynes Sound

- extra small to medium
- creamy, sweet, and briny

STELLAR BAY
Deep Bay, Vancouver Island

- extra small to small
- creamy and fruity with low salinity

Brandy-Glazed Shrimp
with Horseradish Cocktail Sauce

SERVES 4 AND
MAKES 1½ CUPS
OF SAUCE

Cocktail sauce

1 (5½ oz/156 ml)
   can tomato paste
⅓ cup prepared
   horseradish
2 Tbsp honey
2 Tbsp lime juice
2 Tbsp extra virgin olive oil
1 Tbsp Worcestershire
   sauce
1½ tsp Sriracha hot sauce
   or Tabasco

Shrimp

2 Tbsp salted butter
1 Tbsp extra virgin olive oil
3 garlic cloves, minced
1 lb cleaned shrimp, shells
   and tails still attached
2 Tbsp honey
2 Tbsp brandy

The staple cocktail party appetizer, but with a bit of a refresh. Homemade cocktail sauce really does make the difference in this recipe. It is tart, bright with the addition of lime, slightly spicy, and not laden with ketchup. The shrimp have a depth and sweetness from the honey and brandy that is only enhanced when they're dunked into the sauce. Say hello to your new potluck favourite. —EL

To make the cocktail sauce, place all the ingredients in a mixing bowl and whisk together until fully combined. Store in an airtight container in the fridge until ready to use, or for up to 1 month.

To make the shrimp, in a skillet over medium heat, warm the butter and oil. Add the garlic and stir until it starts to sizzle. Add the shrimp and sauté for about 2 minutes, just until they begin to turn pink and start to curl. Drizzle the honey overtop, stirring continuously so the shrimp are well coated and the honey melts. Remove from the heat and pour the brandy into one side of the pan. Be careful, as the alcohol could flare up. Return to the heat and cook for another minute. The sauce will have reduced and the shrimp will be bright pink, tightly curled, and glazed with the sauce.

Serve immediately with the cocktail sauce on the side for dipping.

The shrimp will keep in an airtight container in the fridge for up to 2 days.

Peel-and-Eat Spot Prawns

with Mint Yogurt Dip

Prawns

2 Tbsp celery seeds

2 Tbsp coarse sea salt

4 tsp ground black pepper

4 tsp chili flakes

4 tsp smoked paprika

2 tsp dried English mustard

1 tsp ground nutmeg

1 tsp ground cinnamon

3 quarts water

1 bottle (12 oz / 355 ml)
of your favourite lager
or ale

4 garlic cloves

3 bay leaves

8 whole cloves

2–3 lb prawns (26–30 per
pound), shells split and
deveined

Dip

1½ cups full-fat Greek
yogurt

½ cup finely chopped
fresh mint leaves

1 tsp honey

½ tsp dried English
mustard

Flaked sea salt and ground
black pepper

Spot prawn season in Vancouver Island's waters only lasts 4–6 weeks (early May to late June), so when we can get them fresh, we eat as many as we can possible ingest. This is my favourite way to enjoy them: cooking them as quickly as possible and eating them straight from the shell. —DLA

To prepare the prawns, place the celery seeds, salt, pepper, chili flakes, paprika, dried mustard, nutmeg, and cinnamon in a small bowl and mix to combine.

Fill a large saucepan with the water. Add the spice mix, followed by the lager, garlic, bay leaves, and cloves. Bring to a rolling boil over high heat and boil for at least 5 minutes.

Fill a colander with ice and place it inside a large bowl. Place the prawns in the boiling water. Watch them carefully—they cook quickly and you don't want to overcook them. They are ready when they float and are pink throughout.

Remove the prawns from the water with a slotted spoon and immediately put them into the colander of ice. Put the colander and its bowl in the fridge.

To make the dip, place the yogurt, mint, honey, dried mustard, and a pinch of salt and pepper in a small bowl. Mix well and refrigerate covered until needed.

Serve the prawns alongside the mint yogurt dip. Eat these the day you make them.

sea

Boiled Crab Legs
with Roasted Garlic Butter Dip

SERVES 2

Roasted Garlic Butter Dip
1 large garlic bulb,
   unpeeled
1 Tbsp extra virgin olive oil
½ cup butter
Flaked sea salt

Crab Legs
6 quarts clean sea water
2 Dungeness crabs (about
   5 lb in total), cleaned
   and halved
3 Tbsp coarse sea salt (if
   not using ocean water)

One of the great pleasures of the islands in summer is pulling up a full crab trap and partaking in a beachside boil. I love to cook over an open fire, but when the bans hit, you can still enjoy cooking on the sand with a large propane burner. The butter can be made at home ahead of time and warmed just before serving the crab. —DLA

Preheat the oven to 375°F.

Remove the papery outside layer of the garlic. Cut about ¼ inch from the top of the bulb to expose the cloves. Drizzle the oil over the exposed cloves. Wrap the bulb in aluminum foil and place on a rimmed baking sheet. Bake for 30–40 minutes, or until the garlic cloves are soft and a deep caramel colour. Let cool slightly and remove the cloves from the bulb husk.

In a medium saucepan over medium heat, melt the butter. Using the back of a fork, mash the cloves into the butter. Mix in a pinch of salt. Remove from the heat and pour into a small container and refrigerate until needed. Reheat right before serving.

Fill a large stockpot with the sea water (or 6 quarts water and 3 Tbsp sea salt if you're cooking at home) and bring to a boil over high heat. Place the crab legs in the boiling water and cover the pot with a lid. Cook the crab for 10 minutes, remove from the water, and serve immediately with hot roasted garlic butter.

Leftover crab will keep in an airtight container in the fridge for 2–3 days, and is perfect in the Creamy Crab, Caraway Jill, and Black Kale Dip (page 244). The butter will keep in an airtight container in the fridge for about 1 month.

sea

Grandma's Crab Louis

SERVES 6

4 Tbsp extra virgin olive
  oil, divided
1 small white onion, diced
2 celery stalks, diced
½ tsp sea salt
1 Tbsp lemon juice
¼ cup all-purpose flour
1 cup whipping (35%)
  cream or whole milk
2 cups cooked red rock
  crab
1 tsp cracked black pepper
Finely chopped parsley or
  chives, for garnish

Nowadays, Crab Louis is typically served as a salad, although my grand-mother never made it that way. This rich cream sauce packed with crab was usually served on toast for a decadent brunch after an overflowing crab trap had been pulled up the night before. Serve this over pasta or on toast like Grandma did. It's also lovely over crab cakes, or even steak. —EL

In a small saucepan over medium heat, heat 2 Tbsp of the oil, then add the onion and celery and sauté until just translucent, about 3 minutes. Sprinkle with the salt and continue to sauté, letting the vegetables sweat a little, about 2 minutes. Add the lemon juice and scrape up any bits that have stuck to the pan.

Add the remaining 2 Tbsp oil, sprinkle with flour, and mix well to make a roux. Slowly add the cream, stirring constantly to prevent any lumps from forming. Turn down the heat and continue to stir until you have a rich, thick sauce. Mix in the crab meat, remove from the heat, sprinkle with pepper, and mix gently. Transfer to a serving bowl and sprinkle with parsley or spoon over toast and garnish with parsley.

This will keep in an airtight container in the fridge for up to 2 days.

Brown Butter Scallops

with Crispy Sage Risotto

SERVES 4

8 cups chicken stock
6–8 saffron threads
2 large shallots
2 garlic cloves
½ cup salted butter,
  divided
2 Tbsp extra virgin olive oil
1 tsp fine sea salt, plus
  additional salt to finish
  the dish
1 tsp cracked black pepper,
  plus additional pepper to
  finish the dish
2 cups Arborio rice
1 cup sparkling wine or dry
  white wine
4 sage sprigs, leaves only
12–16 sea scallops
¾ cup grated Parmesan
  cheese, plus extra cheese
  for garnishing the dish

Qualicum Beach and Courtney are home to most of Vancouver Island's scallop beds. Wild BC scallops are smaller than and not as sweet as their East Coast cousins, but they're packed with a rich, complex nutty flavour. The most common varieties found here are pink and spiny. When seared in brown butter, these are crisp on the outside and soft on the inside, sweet and tender, and with a lovely nutty aftertaste. Paired with a subtle and soft risotto, this meal is one for the ages. —EL

In a saucepan over medium-low heat, warm the stock with the saffron.

Finely mince the shallots and garlic—the pieces should be smaller than a grain of rice.

In a large skillet over medium heat, place 2 Tbsp of the butter and the oil. Sauté the shallots and garlic until just translucent, about 2 minutes. Stir in the salt and pepper, letting the shallots and garlic sweat. Add the rice and stir constantly so that it absorbs the butter and oil. It will turn translucent and be quite glossy. Still stirring constantly, gradually add the wine, letting the rice absorb it. The wine will bubble up.

Once the wine has been fully absorbed by the rice, begin to add the stock. Stirring constantly again, add one ladleful of stock at time, letting the rice fully absorb each addition before adding the next. Do this until there are two to three ladles' worth of stock left and the rice is tender and soft yet still textured. You don't want goopy risotto but it shouldn't be crunchy either. Remove from the heat and set aside. Keep the stock warm.

In a separate skillet over medium heat, melt the remaining 6 Tbsp butter. Keep it over the heat until it starts to sizzle, about 2 minutes. Then, watching it constantly and swirling the pan occasionally, let the butter bubble and cook until it turns a lovely brown colour and smells nutty. Pour half the brown butter into a small serving jug.

Leave the rest of the butter in the pan and place it over low heat. Add the sage leaves. They will sizzle and crisp quickly, so act fast. Using tongs, turn them over and then remove from the heat. Each sage leaf only needs 10–15 seconds to crisp. Set aside.

Increase the heat to medium. Pat dry the scallops, and place three to four in the pan to sear, being careful not to crowd the pan. Sear them for 1–2 minutes per side, until well browned and crisp on the outside and no longer translucent on the inside (cut into one to check). Repeat with the remaining scallops. Set aside.

Warm the risotto over medium heat. It will have congealed a bit while you were preparing the sage and scallops, but that's okay. Pour in one ladleful of warm stock and stir to incorporate it into the risotto.

(Continued on page 265)

sea

(Continued from page 263)

After the risotto has loosened a bit, add half a ladleful of stock and the cheese. Stir well to combine and allow the cheese to melt. Remove from the heat and immediately transfer to a serving platter. Top with the scallops and crispy sage leaves, drizzle with the reserved brown butter, season to taste with salt and pepper, and garnish with extra Parmesan, if desired.

The risotto will keep in an airtight container in the fridge for up to 3 days and can be reheated with a little stock. The sage and scallops are best enjoyed the day they are made.

Tomato and Vodka Cream Seafood Pasta

SERVES 4

16 large prawns, peeled

8 scallops

8 mussels

8 clams

2 large shallots

1½ cups cherry tomatoes

½ cup extra virgin olive oil, divided

2 Tbsp chopped basil leaves, plus more chopped basil for garnish

3 tsp chopped oregano leaves, plus more chopped oregano for garnish

2 tsp chopped thyme leaves, plus more thyme leaves for garnish

1½ tsp coarse sea salt, divided

1 tsp ground black pepper

½ tsp chili flakes, plus more chili flakes for garnish

½ cup vodka, divided

¼ cup full-fat cream cheese, cubed

2 cups table (18%) cream

1 (6 oz) can tomato paste

½ lb fettuccini or other long-noodled pasta

½ cup water

Not quite Alfredo, not quite red sauce, rosé sauces are rich and creamy, and full of flavour, richness, and spice. When paired with seafood, they are second to none. The buttery, sweet flavour and texture of local fresh shellfish pairs perfectly with the acidic tomatoes; dry, tart vodka; and herb-forward cream. —EL

Clean all your shellfish (see page 246) and refrigerate until needed.

Preheat the oven to 425°F. Line a rimmed baking sheet with parchment paper.

Roughly chop the shallots, halve the cherry tomatoes, and spread them all on the prepared baking sheet. Drizzle with 2 Tbsp of the oil and gently tip the baking sheet to coat everything evenly.

Using a mortar and pestle, grind the basil, oregano, and thyme with ¾ tsp of the sea salt to a paste-like consistency. Mix in ¼ cup oil and stir to combine. Drizzle over the tomatoes and shallots. Sprinkle with the pepper and chili flakes. Shake the pan again to ensure the herbs are evenly distributed.

Roast for 20 minutes. Remove from the oven and, using a spatula, turn the tomatoes and shallots over so they cook evenly. Roast for another 15 minutes.

Meanwhile, in a saucepan over medium heat, melt the cream cheese, stirring constantly. When it has almost completely melted, gradually whisk in the cream. Whisk in the tomato paste, then slowly pour in the vodka.

For a smooth sauce, let the roasted tomatoes and shallots cool slightly for 2-3 minutes, then blend them with all their cooking juices until smooth. For a chunky sauce, pour the tomatoes, shallots, and the cooking juices into the pan of tomato cream sauce. Stirring constantly, increase the heat to medium-high and let the mixture come to a slow boil. Reduce to your desired consistency. Remove from the heat. At this point, you can store the cooled sauce in an airtight container in the fridge for up to 1 week.

When you're almost ready to serve, bring a large saucepan of salted water to a boil over high heat and cook the pasta until al dente.

Place a small skillet over medium heat and add the remaining oil. Add the prawns and scallops to the pan, sprinkle with the remaining salt, and fry until golden, 1–2 minutes per side. Set aside. Add the water to the pan and place it over high heat. Add the mussels and clams, cover, bring to a boil, and cook for 2–3 minutes, until the shells have opened. Discard any shellfish whose shells don't open.

Place the sauce back over medium heat, add the seafood, and mix gently. Add the cooked pasta and, using tongs, coat it evenly in the sauce. Heat until just starting to bubble. Garnish with herbs and chili flakes.

sea

Cranberry-Glazed Sablefish

2 Tbsp salted butter

1 shallot, sliced into rounds

1 tsp fine sea salt

1 cup fresh cranberries

1 lemon, zested and juiced

½ cup packed brown sugar

¼ cup sherry vinegar

2 bay leaves

4 sprigs thyme

1 sprig rosemary

4 (6 oz each) sablefish
    fillets

Sablefish, also known as black cod, is such a great option if you're wanting to introduce more fish into your diet. It's high in omega-3s and not too fishy taste-wise. Cranberries are grown on Vancouver Island from north of Duncan to Ladysmith. Our local cranberries are a variety of white, pink, and red—often ombré, actually. Tart but not bitter, they make a perfect glaze for this fish. — EL

In a saucepan over low heat, melt the butter. When it starts to sizzle, add the sliced shallots and salt. Caramelize them, stirring occasionally, about 5 minutes. Add the cranberries. They will start to pop after a few minutes. Add the lemon zest and juice, followed by the sugar, vinegar, and herbs. Simmer until the mixture can coat the back of a spoon and the berries have burst. Remove from the heat to cool completely.

Discard the thyme and rosemary sprigs and press the sauce through a fine-mesh sieve into a bowl. Discard the pulp and reserve ⅓ of the strained sauce.

Dry the fillets, place them in an airtight container, pour in the remaining sauce, and turn to coat. Marinate in the fridge overnight, or up to 24 hours, turning once to coat again.

To cook, preheat the broiler to high. Place the oven rack on the second-highest level. Line a baking sheet with parchment paper.

Place the fish on the prepared baking sheet, skin side down. Brush the tops with any residue marinade. Broil for 3–4 minutes, until the tops are caramelized. Turn off the broiler and preheat the oven to 400°F, leaving the fish in the oven while it heats. Leave in the oven for 5–8 minutes after you turn the broiler off. Check the fish to ensure it is opaque. Serve immediately with the reserved sauce on the side.

The sauce will keep in an airtight container in the fridge for 1 week or can be frozen for up to 3 months. The fish is best enjoyed the day it's made.

sea

Whole Grilled Rockfish
with Roasted Tomato Butter

½ lb cherry tomatoes, cut in half, stems removed

2 Tbsp extra virgin olive oil, plus extra for rubbing

Flaked sea salt

½ cup unsalted butter, room temperature

2 lb whole rockfish, scales, guts, and gills removed

One of my favourite things to do when out fishing is to find a nice quiet rocky cove and throw a cod line down. The assortment of rockfish available to us here on Vancouver Island is astounding, and fishing for them always reminds me of that carnival game where kids drop a line over a sheet and pull up a surprise. If fishing isn't an option for you, our local fishmongers always carry a good selection as well. —DLA

Preheat the oven to 300°F. Line a rimmed baking sheet with parchment paper.

Place the cherry tomatoes in a small bowl with the 2 Tbsp oil and a pinch of salt, toss to coat completely, and lay them cut side down on the prepared baking sheet. Roast for 25 minutes, turn them over, and roast for another 25 minutes.

Place the tomatoes and any pan juices in a food processor along with the butter. Pulse repeatedly to blend well. Place a 10-inch square of parchment paper on a work surface and turn the butter out onto it, forming a log about 6 inches long. Roll the parchment tightly around it, twist the ends closed, and place the butter in the fridge or freezer for 30 minutes to an hour to harden.

Meanwhile, wash the fish well and make three to five slashes in the meat perpendicular to the backbone on each side of the fish. If you have a particularly sharp rockfish, snip away the dangerous fins with a pair of kitchen shears. Rub the whole fish with oil and sprinkle liberally with good quality flaked sea salt.

Take the tomato butter from the fridge and cut six 1-inch-thick rounds from it.

Preheat a charcoal or gas grill to about 450°F. You want it to be really hot. Brush the hot grill with a little oil and immediately place the fish on it. Cook for about 5 minutes on each side per inch of thickness. So, a 1-inch-thick fish will need 5 minutes per side. Check the flesh near the side slashes to ensure that it is thoroughly cooked. The flesh should look light and flaky.

Place the grilled fish on a platter. Slip three rounds of butter inside the fish and pop three on top. It should melt into the cuts you made and down into the fish. Serve immediately.

This is best eaten the day it's cooked.

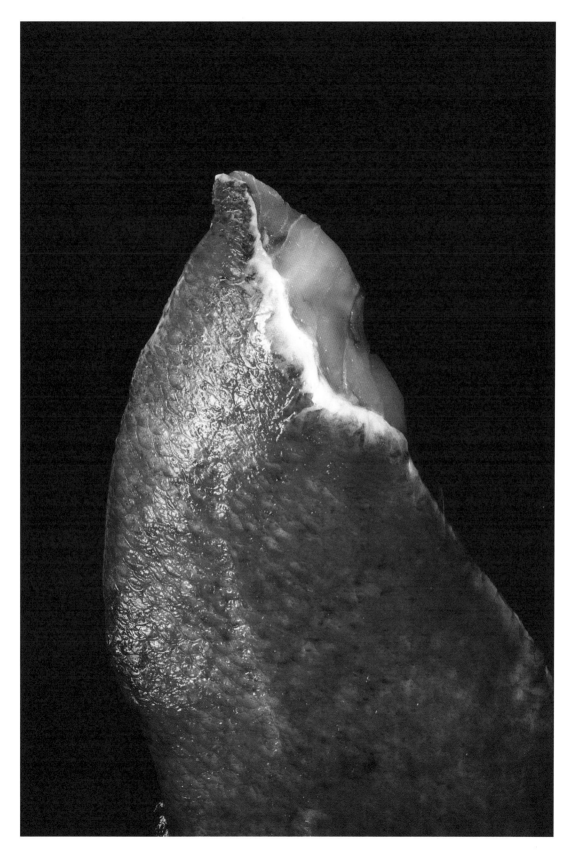

sea

Cedar-Grilled Salmon Steaks
with Cedar-Infused Sea Salt

SERVES 4

Salmon
2 cedar planks (each about
    12 inches long)
4 salmon steaks (6 oz each)
½ cup salted butter
1 Tbsp pure maple syrup
2 tsp lemon juice
1 tsp creamy Dijon
    mustard

Cedar salt
2 small cedar leaf branches
½ cup flaked sea salt
1 tsp ground green
    peppercorns

Making savoury salts is a great way to add a special twist to a dish, and it's fun! Using spruce, cedar, or fir adds a unique flavor to your salt, and will have your guests guessing. I love grilling salmon on cedar, although the short cooking time doesn't allow the cedar to really impart its flavour fully. Topping with some cedar salt creates a well-rounded finish. —EL

Submerge the cedar planks in clean water to soak for at least 1 hour, and up to 24 hours.

Preheat a charcoal or gas grill to high.

Wash the salmon and discard any bones. Pat the salmon dry.

Remove the cedar planks from the water and dry thoroughly. Place two salmon steaks on each piece of wood, 1 inch apart, with 6–8 inches of space at one end for the cedar branches.

In a small bowl, whisk together the butter, maple syrup, lemon juice, and Dijon. Dot the top of the salmon with the butter so it soaks in as the salmon cooks.

To make the cedar salt, wash and dry the cedar branches and discard any large stems. Place them in an even layer in a small heatproof dish on the side of the plank you reserved.

Place the planks on the grill rack and turn off the burner directly under the wood. Close the lid and cook for 18–20 minutes, or until the internal temperature of the salmon is 135°F.

Remove the planks from the grill. Using a sharp knife, finely chop the cedar branches. Grind them with the salt and peppercorns in a mortar using a pestle. Place each salmon steak on a serving plate and top with a sprinkle of cedar salt. Place the remaining salt on the table.

Any salmon leftovers will keep in an airtight container in the fridge for up to 3 days. The cedar salt will keep in an airtight container at room temperature for up to 3 months.

Herb Butter-Broiled Salmon Fillets

SERVES 4

1 cup unsalted butter,
    room temperature
¼ cup chopped tarragon
    leaves
¼ cup chopped flat-leaf
    parsley
¼ cup chopped dill
4 (4 oz each) salmon fillets,
    skin on
Flaked sea salt and cracked
    black pepper
1 lemon, sliced into
    4 wedges

For as far back as I can remember, this has been my favourite way to eat salmon. My dad just chops the herbs, places them on the salmon, squeezes a bit of lemon overtop, and tops it all with butter before popping the salmon in the oven. I like to make an herb compound butter first so that I always have some in the fridge for whenever I get a craving for this dish. —DLA

Place the butter and herbs in a food processor and pulse until the herbs are finely chopped and well combined. Transfer to an airtight container and refrigerate until ready to use.

Place an oven rack 6 inches below the oven broiler and set the heat to high. Line a rimmed baking sheet with aluminium foil.

Place the salmon, skin side down, on the prepared baking sheet. Sprinkle the fillets with a pinch of salt and pepper, top with 1 Tbsp of the herb butter, and broil for 8 minutes. Let rest for 3–4 minutes before serving.

To serve, run a spatula between the fish and the skin to separate the two. Garnish each fillet with a lemon wedge.

Leftover salmon will keep in an airtight container in the fridge for up to 5 days (and makes a great sandwich filling). The butter can be stored in the freezer for up to 3 months.

sea

Hazelnut-Crusted Halibut

with Apricot Habanero Coulis

Apricot Habanero Coulis
6 fresh apricots
1 habanero pepper
¼ cup pure maple syrup
2 Tbsp lemon juice

Halibut
1 cup whole hazelnuts, divided
¼ cup extra virgin olive oil
2 tsp grated lemon zest
1 tsp grated ginger
½ tsp ground cumin
4 (6 oz each) halibut fillets
2 Tbsp Dijon mustard

If I happen to have a favourite kitchen trick, especially to surprise guests, it's combining ingredients that you wouldn't necessarily associate with each other. For example, fresh local hazelnuts, with their creamy, soft texture, seem like a natural ingredient for baking. But when they're roasted, crushed, and mixed with herbs, they make the most tender crust for halibut. Paired with freshly picked apricots and spicy habaneros from the Cowichan Valley, this dish will keep you on your toes from start to finish. —EL

Slice the apricots in half and discard the pits. Finely chop the apricots and place them in a small saucepan over medium heat. Slice the habanero pepper in half, discard the stem and all the seeds, and add it to the pot. Add the maple syrup and lemon juice, and bring to a simmer. Cover and simmer for 5 minutes, until the apricots are very soft. Remove from the heat and discard the habanero, unless you want an extra-spicy sauce. Purée the apricots in the blender to form a thin sauce. Return the sauce to the pan and increase the heat to medium-high. Bring it just to a boil, then turn down the heat and simmer, uncovered, for 5 minutes, stirring to ensure it doesn't stick. When the coulis easily coats the back of a spoon, remove from the heat and transfer to a bowl or jug to cool.

Preheat the oven to 400°F. Line a rimmed baking sheet with parchment paper.

In a dry skillet, toast the hazelnuts over medium heat, gently swirling and shaking the pan to rotate them, until fragrant and golden, 3–4 minutes. Transfer to a food processor and pulse until they look like a coarse flour. You want an even consistency, without any big chunks of nuts. Place them in a small bowl and drizzle in the oil, mixing once just to coat them. Add the lemon zest, ginger, and cumin. Mix well to evenly distribute the spices.

Place the halibut on the prepared baking sheet. Brush the top of each fillet evenly with the Dijon. Divide the hazelnut mixture evenly among the tops of the fillets, pressing down to make a firm crust. Bake for 8–10 minutes, until the fish has an internal temperature of 140°F, is fully opaque inside, and easily flakes with a fork. Remove from the oven and transfer to a serving platter. Drizzle with some coulis and serve with extra coulis on the side.

The fish will keep in an airtight container in the fridge for up to 3 days. The coulis will keep in an airtight container in the fridge for up to 2 weeks.

Grilled Oolichan
with Tarragon Mayo

SERVES 4

2 lemons
¼ cup extra virgin olive oil
2 Tbsp lemon juice
1 clove garlic, minced
2 tsp red chilli flakes
1 tsp grated lemon zest
1 tsp flaked sea salt
20 fresh small (4–5 inches long each) smelt, heads on
1 cup full-fat mayonnaise
¼ cup chopped tarragon leaves
1 tsp apple cider vinegar

I grew up knowing these fish by their West Coast First Nations name, oolichan or candlefish, but they are also commonly known as Pacific smelt. These fish were important to coastal people as they're extremely high in oil, so much so that they can be burned as candles when dried. They also make good eating fish. My dad loves them in place of his traditional English kippers for breakfast, and I love them as a light supper with a vinegary potato salad. When small, they can be grilled whole and eaten in their entirety, but any bigger than 6 inches should be cleaned first. —DLA

Cut the lemons in half widthwise and set aside.

In a 13- × 9-inch baking dish, mix together the oil, lemon juice, garlic, chilli flakes, lemon zest, and salt. Add the smelt to this marinade and refrigerate, covered, for at least 30 minutes, or up to 1 hour.

Heat a charcoal or gas grill to medium-high. Place the smelt directly on the grill. Place the lemons, cut side down, on the grill as well. Cook the smelt for 4–5 minutes per side, or until a deep golden brown.

In a mixing bowl, whisk together the mayo, tarragon, and vinegar. Refrigerate until you're ready to serve.

Remove the fish from the grill and squeeze the juice from the grilled lemons overtop. Serve immediately with the tarragon mayonnaise on the side.

Halibut Fillets
with Fire-Roasted Field Salsa

SERVES 4

6 medium on-the-vine or
Roma tomatoes, halved

2 red bell peppers, halved,
deseeded

4–6 jalapeño peppers,
halved, deseeded

2 red onions, halved

¼ cup extra virgin olive oil

4 large cloves garlic, peeled
but left whole

4 (each 4–6 oz) halibut
fillets

½ cup dry white wine

1 bunch cilantro, roughly
chopped

1 lime, juiced

1 (5½ oz/156 ml) can
tomato paste

Coarse sea salt

4 Tbsp salted butter

Ground black pepper

Halibut is a Vancouver Island staple. This bottom-feeding fish is quite remarkable. Because they live on the ocean floor, they don't need to look down, so sometimes their eyes migrate to one side of their head. They even swim sideways. These fish are very large and the fillets are meaty and flavourful but they're not overly fishy. Their thickness makes them ideal for cooking on an open grill. A good rule of thumb is 8 minutes per inch of thickness of fish. —EL

Heat a charcoal or gas grill to high.

Toss the tomatoes, peppers, and onions in the oil, coating them well. Place a garlic clove in each bell pepper half.

Place the halibut on a large plate and drizzle the fillets with the wine. Refrigerate while you make the salsa.

Place the vegetables on the grill, cut side up.

Turn down the grill to medium and let the vegetables cook until well charred, 15 minutes. Using tongs, transfer them to a blender.

Add the cilantro and lime juice to the blender. Blend to your desired consistency. Pour the salsa into a bowl, whisk in the tomato paste, and season to taste with salt. Refrigerate while you prepare the halibut.

While the grill is still hot, brush it clean and oil it so the fillets don't stick. Place the fillets on it immediately. Place 1 Tbsp of butter on each fillet, close the lid, and cook for 5–8 minutes, or until the internal temperature is 140°F and the flesh is fully opaque and easily flakes apart with a fork.

Remove the halibut from the grill and place on serving plates. Serve with a spoonful of fresh salsa overtop each fillet.

The cooked halibut will keep refrigerated in an airtight container for up to 2 days. The salsa will keep in an airtight container in the fridge for up to 1 month.

sea

Green Tea and Blue Algae Ice Cream

MAKES 4 CUPS

2 Tbsp green tea leaves
½ cup just-boiling water
¼ cup full fat cream cheese
¼ cup cornstarch
1 cup granulated sugar
2 cups whole milk
1 cup whipping (35%)
   cream
¼ cup blue algae powder

Kids love blue raspberry freezies, although the amount of artificial dyes that are added to create that special colour makes me shudder. The good news is that ice cream can be florescent blue and additive-free. Our incredible oceans give us so much—including blue algae to create this kid-friendly, fun, tasty ice cream! Making it egg free keeps the colour bright. Blue algae is found in most health food stores on Vancouver Island. Westholme Tea Farm's Green Dragon tea is my favourite for this, but any green tea will work well. —EL

Prepare your ice cream maker as per the manufacturer's instructions.

Steep the tea in the just-boiling water for an extra-concentrated brew.

In a saucepan over medium-low heat, gently melt the cream cheese. In a small bowl, whisk together the cornstarch and sugar until lump-free. Add cornstarch and sugar mixture and the milk and the cream to the pan. Whisk to combine. Strain the tea and add to the pan. Whisking constantly, bring it to a boil. Boil for 1 minute, then remove from the heat. Mix the blue algae with 2 Tbsp of water and add to the pan, whisking to create an even colour. Pour into a bowl, cover with plastic wrap, making sure it touches the surface to prevent a skin from forming. Refrigerate for at least 4 hours, or overnight.

Remove from the fridge, uncover, and stir the chilled base. Follow the manufacturer's instructions to churn the ice cream. Spoon the ice cream into a 9- × 5-inch loaf pan and place in the freezer for at least 2–3 hours.

The ice cream will keep in an airtight container in the freezer for up to 3 months.

sea

Dark Chocolate Nori Bark

SERVES 4–6

20–30 nori snack sheets, cut into thin strips

1 cup whole tamari almonds

10 oz bittersweet chocolate, finely chopped, divided

1 Tbsp 100% vegetable shortening

1 tsp pure vanilla extract

Flaked sea salt

There's something about salty chocolate that is just so incredibly delicious—and very more-ish. Being a West Coast island girl, I love sushi and all things nori, so I created this little treat using tamari almonds and seaweed for when my sweet tooth wants chocolate. The base of this will work with every topping, so if you prefer your nuts without the nori, that will work as well. —DLA

Line a 13- × 9-inch rimmed baking sheet with parchment paper, allowing the paper to hang over the edges so that the chocolate is easier to remove when it's set.

Evenly spread half of the nori strips and half of the almonds across the pan. Set aside.

In a double boiler or in a stainless steel bowl set overtop of a saucepan with 1–2 inches of gently simmering water, melt half of the chocolate with the shortening. Remove from the heat and stir in the remaining chocolate until it too is fully melted. Add the vanilla and stir to combine.

Slowly pour the chocolate onto the baking sheet in an even layer, spreading it gently with a spatula to get the top surface fairly smooth. Top with the remaining nori and almonds, gently pressing them into the melted chocolate with the edge of a spoon. Sprinkle with 2 pinches of salt.

Let the bark sit for up to 90 minutes, or until firmly set. Once it's firm, use a large knife to cut it into pieces, or cover it with more parchment and shatter it with your fingers.

This will keep in an airtight container at room temperature for up to 2 weeks.

sea

Spruced-Up Caesars Three Ways

SERVES 4

Clamato-style base
4 on-the-vine tomatoes
2 large red bell peppers
1 clove garlic
1 shallot
2 Tbsp extra virgin olive oil
1 tsp celery seeds
1 tsp sea salt
½ tsp cracked black pepper
1 cup clam juice
Celery salt for rimming
　the glasses
Ice cubes

In many ways there isn't a more classic Canadian cocktail. Between the clam juice, tomatoes, celery, and hot sauce, you really have something from almost every province in the mix! Spice it up with fun garnishes, from pickled beans and cucumber dills, to bacon, to the classic stalk of celery. You can get pretty adventurous with them. Here are three of my favourite ways to make a Caesar. They all start with the same homemade base. (Note: Want to make it green? Substitute 6 tomatillos for the tomatoes.) —EL

Preheat the oven to 375°F. Line a rimmed baking sheet with parchment paper.

Slice the tomatoes into ½-inch thick rounds and spread them evenly over the baking sheet. Quarter the peppers vertically, discarding the seeds, and nestle them into the tomatoes. Crush the garlic and quarter the shallot and add them to the pan. Drizzle the oil overtop and sprinkle with the celery seeds, salt, and pepper.

Roast for 25 minutes, until the vegetables are well roasted and the pan is filled with juices. Remove from the oven and let rest for 5 minutes.

Pour the entire contents of the pan, including the juices, into a blender and purée until completely smooth. Add the clam juice and blend again. Pour the mixture through a mesh strainer into a large mason jar or pitcher to remove any extra pulp and refrigerate to cool completely before using.

To make each of the variations, in a large cocktail shaker containing a few ice cubes, add the Clamato-stye base and all the other ingredients (except garnishes, of course!). Shake well to combine. Rim four Tom Collins glasses with celery salt, if desired, and half-fill with ice cubes. Divide the liquid in the shaker between the glasses and garnish as desired.

Classic Caesar

2 cups Clamato-style base (see page 288)
4 oz vodka
2 oz lime juice
2 tsp Worcestershire sauce
1 tsp Tabasco sauce
2 Tbsp celery salt
4 lime wedges, for garnish
4 stalks celery, for garnish

Seafood Special

8 cooked cocktail shrimp (put 2 shrimp each
on 4 skewers)
2 cups Clamato-style base (see page 288)
4 oz vodka
2 oz lemon juice
2 tsp horseradish (not creamy style)
1 tsp Worcestershire sauce
½ tsp Sriracha hot sauce
2 Tbsp celery salt
4 lemon wedges, for garnish

Bacon Bourbon

2 cups Clamato-style base (see page 288)
4 oz bourbon
1 oz dill pickle juice
2 tsp pure maple syrup
2 tsp Worcestershire sauce
1 tsp Tabasco sauce
2 Tbsp celery salt
4 strips cooked thick-cut bacon, for garnish
4 lemon wedges, for garnish
4 large dill pickles, for garnish

DIY Sea Salt

5 gallons clean sea water

Although it is obviously much easier to go to the store and buy salt (and there are many fabulous sea salt producers on Vancouver Island), there is something really special about making it. So, for kicks and giggles, here is how to make sea salt at home. On average the salt solution of the Pacific Ocean is about 5%, so for every 4 cups of water, you'll yield about 1 tablespoon of salt. Try to use water from an area with strong currents so it is clean and fresh. –EL

Strain the water through a cheesecloth-lined sieve to remove any sand.

Fill a shallow skillet three-quarters full with sea water. Bring to a simmer, uncovered, over medium heat and watch the steam rise. There's no need to watch it like a hawk; just keep an eye on it. As the water evaporates, start to replenish it with the remaining sea water. Allowing the water to steam off and not boil allows the salt to form larger crystals and also prevents scorching. This process will take several hours, even a day. As you start to see salt form at the bottom of the pan, stir gently once or twice to ensure it's not sticking. The water will look a bit snowy, with salt forming at the bottom. Gently start to pull the salt to one side, making a little pile and allowing more surface area for the water to steam off. When only ¼ cup of water is left, remove the pan from the heat.

Preheat the oven to 150°F, or as low as it can go. Line a baking sheet with parchment paper.

Carefully spoon the salt onto the baking sheet in an even layer. Don't break the crystals but do gently break up any clumps. Dry in the oven for 30–45 minutes, shaking the pan gently every 15 minutes, until all the water has evaporated. Allow the salt to cool completely. Transfer carefully to a bowl or dish and enjoy.

This will keep in an airtight container at room temperature for up to one year (although I've never had salt go bad).

sea

Acknowledgements

To James and the children: Thank you for always allowing our home and kitchen to be ground zero throughout my creative process and for infusing the days with much laughter, music, and merriment. To dear Emily: Thank you for always creating the most incredibly delicious food—with you in the kitchen every meal is a celebration and life just tastes better when you're around. To our amazingly talented stylist Aurelia: You turn every dish into a work of art. You make me a better photographer every single day. To my BFF Angie: Can you be my wing woman on these crazy adventures for the rest of our days? And with the fullest heart, Taryn: What can I say? This book was five years of dreaming that all started with you—*thank you* for being the good fairy with the magical wand that turned this crazy wish into reality.—DLA

I would like to thank all of the people who have helped me along the way, as I fell deeper and deeper in love with food, and especially with the way it brings us all closer together. I still can't believe I get to do this for a living. To my husband Stephen: From being the best dishwasher and errand runner right down to counting every piece of charcoal that goes into the barbecue for me, everything you do is so appreciated. I love sharing this adventure with you. To Danielle: Working on this project with you has been a dream come true. Here's to the crazy, long days of shooting, and late nights cleaning the kitchen as James would serenade us with his guitar. Thank you for opening up your home to me, and for making me a better person. To Taryn: Your super-powered publishing team is incredible, and I can't thank them enough for working tirelessly to bring this book to life. —EL

Special thanks, from the both of us, to Gerry Morrison, Erin Morris Ceramics, Terra Nossa Organic Farms, Bullock Lake Farm, Sarah Barrette & Inspired, Ollie's Fishing Charters, Windsor Farms, Rathjen Cellars, End of the Road Farm, Westholme Tea Farm, Francis Bread, McClintock's Farm, True Grain Bread, Weinberg's Good Food, Silver Rill Berry Farm, Starling Lane Vineyard, and Lockwood Farms, without whom this book would never have been as delicious, amazing, beautiful, and insightful as it has been to create.

Resources

Sharing the beauty and bounty of Vancouver Island is one of our favourite things to do, and this section aims to make it easy to discover and appreciate the amazing food this island has to offer.

VANCOUVER ISLAND FARMERS MARKET LIST

One lovely way to find delicious local food on Vancouver Island is to seek out a local farmers market. Many operate year-round—held outdoor in the summer and indoor during the winter months—and others are strictly seasonal. The best part about farmers markets is that the booths are often tended by the farm owners, artisans, or producers themselves. They are so knowledgeable, passionate, and generous in offering suggestions to home cooks and gardeners. Many of the photos and places Danielle and I explored in researching and writing this book began with a conversation at a local market. In fact, most of the ingredients Danielle has photographed so beautifully in these pages were purchased from local markets or from a Community Supported Agriculture (CSA) weekly delivery box. Supporting local farmers, especially Island farmers, is crucial to keeping our economy and community healthy.

One special note: the Cowichan Valley Co-operative (cow-op.ca) is a really unique market. It's an online farmers market where locals who live in the Cowichan Valley and the Capital Region (Victoria and surrounding communities) can order produce online from a wide variety of farmers. The produce is picked to order and delivered weekly to predetermined locations for pickup. This allows you to support producers year-round.

Visit the BC Farmers Market Trail (bcfarmersmarkettrail.com) for the most current and accurate information for the majority of the markets listed below. This site has extensive and updated info on market dates, hours, locations, and parking as well as other handy information, including whether or not the market is dog-friendly, wheelchair-accessible, has an ATM, or is hosting any special events. —EL

South Island

Goldstream Farmers Market	May–October; Saturdays	Langford
Metchosin Farmers Market	May–October; Sundays	Metchosin
North Saanich Farm Market	June–October; Saturdays	Saanich
Peninsula Country Market	June–October; Saturdays	Saanich
Sidney Street Market	June–August; Thursday evenings	Saanich
Sooke Country Market	May–October; Saturdays	Sooke
Esquimalt Farmers Market	May–October; Thursday evenings	Victoria
James Bay Community Market	May–September; Saturdays	Victoria

South Island

Oak Bay Village Market	June–September; second Wednesday evening of each month	Victoria
Oaklands Sunset Market	July–September; Wednesday evenings	Victoria
Moss Street Market	May–October; Saturdays	Victoria

Southern Gulf Islands

Salt Spring Saturday Market	May–October; Saturdays	Ganges
Salt Spring Tuesday Farmers Market	Tuesday afternoons	Ganges
Pender Island Farmers Market	May–August; Saturdays	Pender Island

Cowichan

Chemainus Wednesday Market	May–September; Wednesday evenings	Chemainus
Cobble Hill Farmers Market	June–September; Thursday evenings	Cobble Hill
Duncan Farmers Market	Year-round; Saturdays	Duncan
Honeymoon Bay Market	May–October; Saturdays	Honeymoon Bay

Central Island

Cedar Farmers Market	May–October; Sundays	Cedar
Errington Farmers Market	May–September; Saturdays	Errington
Gabriola Farmers Market	May–October; Saturdays	Gabriola Island
Island Roots Market Co-Op	Year-round; Wednesday evenings	Nanaimo
Nanaimo Downtown Farmers Market	May–September; Saturdays	Nanaimo
Parksville Museum Farmers Market	June–August; Friday evenings	Parksville
Summer by the Sea Street Market	June–August; Tuesday evenings	Parksville
Qualicum Beach Farmers Market	Year-round; Saturdays	Qualicum Beach

Pacific Rim

Spirit Square Farmers Market	Year-round; Saturdays	Port Alberni
Tofino Public Market	May–October; Saturdays	Tofino

North Central Island

Magnolia Court Summer Farm Market	June–August; Wednesday evenings	Bowser
Pier Street Farmers Market and Arts Fair	May–September; Sundays	Campbell River
Comox Valley Farmers Market	Year-round; Saturdays	Comox
Cumberland Farmers Market	July–September; Sundays	Cumberland
Denman Island Farmers Market	May–October; Saturdays	Denman Island
The Merville Hall Gumboot Market	Year-round; Monday evenings	Merville

North Island

North Island Farmers and Artisans Market	April–September; Saturdays	Port Hardy
North Island Farmers and Artisans Market	May–September; Saturdays	Port McNeill

The roots of farm-to-table culture are deep on Vancouver Island. Many chefs work closely with local farmers, asking them to grow unique varieties of fruits and vegetables specifically for their restaurants. Some even have their own farms! Supporting local producers is a priority and a matter of principle for many restaurants on the Island, and it's a core part of their business mandate.

The plethora of farm-to-table restaurants on Vancouver Island is encouraging, and the number of these restaurants is growing steadily. From simple favourites like Big Wheel Burger, a local burger bar, to the delights of 10 Acres Bistro, Olo, and Wolf in the Fog, the list is long. Here we've done our best to compile a list of restaurants that not only support local farmers but also hold true to the farm-to-table philosophy of cooking.

Note that this list may not be exhaustive. It does not include the long list of coffee shops, bakeries, and grocery stores who are committed to supporting our local artisans and producers. Also note that not all of these establishments are restaurants; they may be private farms, vineyards, or even food trucks that are open seasonally or by purchasing a ticket or reserving ahead. Make sure to visit the company's website for information before visiting in person. —EL

South Island

Charlotte and the Quail	charlotteandthequail.ca	Saanich
Fireside Grill	firesidegrill.com	Saanich
The Roost Vineyard Bistro & Farm Bakery	roostfarmcentre.com	Saanich
Harvest Road – Farm to Table Grill	facebook.com/Harvest.rd.farmtotable//	Saanichton
Sooke Harbour House	sookeharbourhouse.com	Sooke
Wild Mountain Food and Drink	wildmountaindinners.com	Sooke
10 Acres Farm and Restaurant Group	10acres.ca	Victoria
Agrius	agriusrestaurant.com	Victoria
Aura Waterfront Restaurant	aurarestaurant.ca	Victoria
Be Love	beloverestaurant.ca	Victoria
The Beach House Restaurant	beachhousevictoria.com	Victoria
Big Wheel Burger	bigwheelburger.com	Victoria
Brasserie L'Ecole	lecole.ca	Victoria
The Courtney Room	thecourtneyroom.com	Victoria
FishHook Restaurants	fishhookvic.com	Victoria
The Livet	thelivet.ca	Victoria
Nourish Kitchen and Café	nourishkitchen.ca	Victoria
OLO Restaurant	olorestaurant.com	Victoria
Part and Parcel	partandparcel.ca	Victoria
Q at the Empress	qattheempress.com	Victoria
Red Fish Blue Fish	redfish-bluefish.com	Victoria
Spinnakers Gastro Brewpub	spinnakers.com	Victoria

resources

South Island

Vista 18 West Coast Grill	vista18.com	Victoria
Zambri's	zambris.ca	Victoria

Gulf Islands

Pilgrimme	pilgrimme.ca	Galiano Island
Bridgemans Bistro	bridgemans.ca	North Pender Island

Cowichan

The Bistro at Cherry Point Estate Wines	cherrypointestatewines.com	Cobble Hill
The Eatery at Merridale	merridale.ca	Cobble Hill
Masthead Restaurant	themastheadrestaurant.com	Cowichan Bay
True Grain Bakery	truegrain.ca	Cowichan Bay
Alderlea Farm Café	alderleafarm.com	Duncan
Deerholme Farm	deerholme.com	Duncan
Hudson's On First	hudsonsonfirst.ca	Duncan
Providence Farm	providencefarm.wildapricot.org	Duncan
Bridgemans Bistro	bridgemans.ca	Mill Bay
Unsworth Vineyards	unsworthvineyards.com	Mill Bay
Farm Table Inn	farmtableinn.ca	Skutz Falls

Central Island

Gabriel's Café	gabrielscafe.ca	Nanaimo
Mahle House Restaurant	mahlehouse.ca	Nanaimo
The Nest Bistro	thenestbistro.com	Nanaimo
Bistro 694	Bistro694.com	Qualicum Beach

Pacific Rim

Pescadores Bistro	pescadores.ca	Port Alberni
Sobo	sobo.ca	Tofino
Wolf in the Fog	wolfinthefog.com	Tofino
Ravenlady	ravenlady.ca	Ucluelet
Zoe's Bakery & Café	zoesbakeryandcafe.com	Ucluelet

North Central Island

Avenue Bistro	avenuebistro.ca	Comox
Local's Restaurant at the Old House	oldhousevillage.com	Courtenay
True Grain Bakery	truegrain.ca	Courtenay

North Island

Northern Lights Restaurant	northernlightsrestaurant.ca	Port McNeill
Bridgemans Bistro	bridgemans.ca	Port Renfrew
Cable Cookhouse	cablecookhouse.ca	Sayward

SUBSTITUTIONS AND REPLACEMENTS

Many of the ingredients included or featured within these pages are either only commonly available on Vancouver Island, or have a very short growing season, or both. Below we've compiled a list of substitutions so you can enjoy this book's recipes all year long, no matter where you live. —EL

If the recipe calls for:	Replace with:
black currants	50/50 mixture blackberries and blueberries
buffalo milk	whole organic milk
delicata squash	acorn squash
garlic scapes	green onions or garlic chives
goat milk	whole organic milk
Herbes de Comox	Herbes de Provence
Little Qualicum Cheeseworks "Caraway Jill" cheese	Monterey Jack Cheese + 1 tsp caraway seeds per cup of grated cheese
Little Qualicum Cheeseworks "Monterey Jill" cheese	Monterey Jack cheese
lobster mushrooms	porcini mushrooms
lovage	50/50 mixture of parsley and arugula
nettles	50/50 mixture of arugula and spinach
Peabody gin	London Dry gin
Red Fife wheat flour	unbleached whole wheat flour
rockfish	lake trout
salal berries	blueberries
Salt Spring Island lamb	lamb from New Zealand or your local farm
spot prawns	jumbo shrimp
tayberries	50/50 mixture blackberries and raspberries
venison	beef or pork
wild morels	porcini mushrooms
wild plums	prune or black plums
Yellow Point cranberries or wild cranberries	fresh or frozen cranberries

Conversions Chart

VOLUME

⅛ tsp	0.5 mL
¼ tsp	1 mL
½ tsp	2.5 mL
¾ tsp	4 mL
1 tsp	5 mL
1 ½ tsp	7.5 mL
2 tsp	10 mL
1 Tbsp	15 mL
4 tsp	20 mL
2 Tbsp	30 mL
3 Tbsp	45 mL
¼ cup / 4 Tbsp	60 mL
5 Tbsp	75 mL
⅓ cup	80 mL
½ cup	125 mL
⅔ cup	160 mL
¾ cup	185 mL
1 cup	250 mL
1 ¼ cups	310 mL
1 ½ cups	375 mL
1 ¾ cups	435 mL
2 cups / 1 pint	500 mL
2 ¼ cups	560 mL
2 ½ cups	625 mL

VOLUME

3 cups	750 mL
3 ½ cups	875 mL
4 cups / 1 quart	1 L
4 ½ cups	1.125 L
5 cups	1.25 L
5 ½ cups	1.375 L
6 cups	1.5 L
6 ½ cups	1.625 L
7 cups	1.75 L
8 cups	2 L
12 cups	3 L
¼ fl oz	7.5 mL
½ fl oz	15 mL
¾ fl oz	22 mL
1 fl oz	30 mL
1 ½ fl oz	45 mL
2 fl oz	60 mL
3 fl oz	90 mL
4 fl oz	125 mL
5 fl oz	160 mL
6 fl oz	185 mL
8 fl oz	250 mL
24 fl oz	750 mL

WEIGHT	
1 oz	30 g
2 oz	60 g
3 oz	90 g
¼ lb / 4 oz	125 g
5 oz	150 g
6 oz	175 g
½ lb / 8 oz	250 g
9 oz	270 g
10 oz	300 g
¾ lb / 12 oz	375 g
14 oz	400 g
1 lb	500 g
1 ½ lb	750 g
2 lb	1 kg
2 ½ lb	1.25 kg
3 lb	1.5 kg
4 lb	1.8 kg
5 lb	2.3 kg
5 ½ lb	2.5 kg
6 lb	2.7 kg

LENGTH	
1/8 inch	3 mm
¼ inch	6 mm
3/8 inch	9 mm
½ inch	1.25 cm
¾ inch	2 cm
1 inch	2.5 cm
1 ½ inches	4 cm
2 inches	5 cm
3 inches	8 cm
4 inches	10 cm
4 ½ inches	11 cm
5 inches	12 cm
6 inches	15 cm
7 inches	18 cm
8 inches	20 cm
8 ½ inches	22 cm
9 inches	23 cm
10 inches	25 cm
11 inches	28 cm
12 inches	30 cm

OVEN TEMPERATURE

40°f	5°c
120°f	49°c
125°f	51°c
130°f	54°c
135°f	57°c
140°f	60°c
145°f	63°c
150°f	66°c
155°f	68°c
160°f	71°c
165°f	74°c
170°f	77°c
180°f	82°c
200°f	95°c
225°f	107°c
250°f	120°c

OVEN TEMPERATURE

275°f	140°c
300°f	150°c
325°f	160°c
350°f	180°c
375°f	190°c
400°f	200°c
425°f	220°c
450°f	230°c
475°f	240°c
500°f	260°c

CAN SIZES

4 oz	114 mL
14 oz	398 mL
19 oz	540 mL
28 oz	796 mL

conversions chart

Index

index

index

314

index

TouchWood Editions
touchwoodeditions.com

The information in this book is true and complete to the best of the authors' knowledge. All recommendations are made without guarantee on the part of the authors or the publisher.

Editing by Lesley Cameron
Design by Tree Abraham
Photography by DL Acken
Food styling by Aurelia Louvet

LIBRARY AND ARCHIVES CANADA CATALOGUING IN PUBLICATION
Title: Cedar + salt : Vancouver Island recipes from forest, farm, field, and sea / DL Acken and Emily Lycopolus.
Other titles: Cedar and salt
Names: Acken, DL (Danielle L.), author, photographer. | Lycopolus, Emily, author.
Description: Includes index.
Identifiers: Canadiana 20190120061 | ISBN 9781771512947 (hardcover)
Subjects: LCSH: Cooking, Canadian—British Columbia style. | LCSH: Local foods—British Columbia—
   Vancouver Island. | LCGFT: Cookbooks.
Classification: LCC TX715.6 .A25 2019 | DDC 641.59711/2—dc23

TouchWood Editions gratefully acknowledges that land on which we live and work is within the traditional territories of the Lkwungen (Esquimalt and Songhees), Malahat, Pacheedaht, Scia'new, T'Sou-ke and W̱SÁNEĆ (Pauquachin, Tsartlip, Tsawout, Tseycum) peoples.

We acknowledge the financial support of the Government of Canada through the Canada Book Fund and, and of the Province of British Columbia through the Book Publishing Tax Credit.

This book was produced using FSC®-certified, acid-free papers, processed chlorine-free and printed with soya-based inks.

Printed in China

23 22 21 20 19   1 2 3 4 5